SOUTHERN AFRICA: PROSPECTS FOR PEACE AND SECURITY

International Peace Academy

Southern Africa: Prospects for Peace and Security

The Second International Conference on Peace and Security in Southern Africa,
Arusha International Conference Centre, United Republic of Tanzania,
2–6 March, 1986

IPA Report No. 25

1987

International Peace Academy
NEW YORK

Martinus Nijhoff Publishers
DORDRECHT / BOSTON / LANCASTER

Distributors

for the United States and Canada: Kluwer Academic Publishers, P.O. Box 358, Accord Station, Hingham, MA 02018-0358, USA
for the UK and Ireland: Kluwer Academic Publishers, MTP Press Limited, Falcon House, Queen Square, Lancaster LA1 1RN, UK
for all other countries: Kluwer Academic Publishers Group, Distribution Center, P.O. Box 322, 3300 AH Dordrecht, The Netherlands

Library of Congress Cataloging in Publication Data

```
International Conference on Peace and Security
   (2nd : 1986 : Arusha International Conference
   Centre)
   Southern Africa : prospects for peace and security.

   1. Africa, Southern--National security--Congresses.
I. International Peace Academy.  II. Title.
UA855.6.I57 1986    355'.033068        86-18097
ISBN 0-89838-920-8
ISBN 0-89838-921-6 (pbk.)
```


ISBN 0-89838-920-8 (Hardback)
ISBN 0-89838-921-6 (Paperback)

Copyright

PRINTED IN THE NETHERLANDS

TABLE OF CONTENTS

FOREWORD

This workshop was first conceived during a conversation with President Julius Nyerere at a meeting of the six heads of state of the Five Continent Peace Initiative held in January 1985 in Athens. During a discussion of the IPA's activities, I sought his advice on the Academy's future plans in Africa.

President Nyerere advised that the Academy was ideally suited to promote regional cooperation and establish communications between all parties involved in the prevailing conflicts in Southern Africa. He emphasized that ouside institutes like the IPA could provide the necessary stimuli for discussions that could contribute to the promotion of peace and understanding. The Second International Conference on Peace and Security in Southern Africa was hosted by the Centre for Foreign Relations of the Ministry of Foreign Affairs of the United Republic of Tanzania and the University of Dar es Salaam, both of a country that prominently supports liberation movements and negotiations. The IPA is most grateful to the Government for supporting this workshop — both financially and logistically. The Centre for Foreign Relations and the University of Dar es Salaam made excellent arrangements and provided valuable resource staff for the workshop.

Negotiating the end of conflicts in Southern Africa presents a formidable challenge for the international community, in particular for the African leadership. The negotiating process demands an understanding of African politics and statesmanship from leaders of other countries with interests in the region, especially the Superpowers.

Ever since 1971, one year after it was established, the

International Peace Academy has organized a number of off-the-record workshops, in the United States, Europe and Africa on the subject of negotiating the end of conflicts in Africa. These were made possible largely by the generous support of the Ford, Rockefeller and McKnight Foundations. Our workshops on Africa have considered the role of the Organization of African Unity, relations between the OAU/UN, conflicts in Chad, Western Sahara, and the process of decolonization in Namibia. In recent years, the Academy has devoted almost one third of its resources to the search for the peaceful resolution of conflicts in Africa. It has published reports on all the workshops, as well as a book, *From Rhodesia to Zimbabwe*. The Academy was also involved in the behind the scences negotiation leading to the independence of Zimbabwe.

The Academy was mainly focused on off-the-record workshops in Southern Africa since the adoption of UN Security Council Resolution 435. On an informal suggestion from special political affairs officers of the UN Secretary-General, two of whom are on our Board of Directors, the Academy undertook a study of Namibia including off-the-record meetings involving all parties concerned, and likely donors to UNTAG.

At the XVIII summit meeting of the heads of state of the OAU held in Nairobi in June 1981, a consensus was arrived at on solutions to Chadian and Western Saharan conflicts. At a pre-ceeding meeting of the OAU Council of Ministers, a Ministerial Committee was set up to consider the proposals for a Peace Council and a Boundaries Commission in unison with the ongoing Charter review. The proposal for a Defence Force was also to be studied. Unfortunately, Africa ran into many of the same problems it has faced since independence, because the continent lacked the resources with which to shoulder such responsibility, or the heavy financial burden.

From the 1980s onwards, the security situation in Southern Africa began to deteriorate. South Africa had embarked on its policy to destabilize neighboring states which provided help to SWAPO and ANC. South African Defence Forces (SADF) invaded Angola. The negotiations being undertaken to resolve the future of Namibia by the Western Five Contact Group were overtaken by the new American Administration's so-called policy of 'constructive engagement' with South Africa.

In the meantime, the OAU operation in Chad had failed, with Libya and France supporting their respective clients in the field. The IPA's review of the OAU's ability to cope with conflicts revealed that after two decades, OAU member states were less concerned with the decolonization process and were divided over the question of Western Sahara. The OAU needed to focus on a new machinery for dealing with inter-state and intra-state conflicts, modalities for negotiating solutions and implementing decisions revolving around peace and security. Regrettably, OAU's progress in dealing with these issues has proved very slow.

By 1984, the OAU members had rallied around the issue of Namibia and South Africa. Prime Minister P.W. Botha, later to be President, had introduced a new constitution to give some voice to the coloreds and the Indians, but not to the blacks because they were being relegated to their homelands. A majority of the coloreds and Indians rejected the offer. The UN's Anti-Apartheid Committee became more vocal. Even the United States was not insulated from the surge of moral questioning; the Reagan Administration's policy of 'constructive engagement' was being questioned by more and more Americans.

In South Africa, black political leaders had become more frustrated and restive. Civil disobedience erupted causing more than a thousand black deaths and many thousands to be injured. There were white deaths too and many casualties amongst the South African security forces.

Early in 1984, the Nkomati and Lusaka Accords gave promise of an end to fighting between South African forces and its neighbors, notably Mozambique and Angola. The accords turned out to be an illusion.

While we were meeting in Arusha, many black South Africans were dying for change and freedom. The heartbeat of apartheid is ebbing — apartheid will die. We thus need to consider how to dismantle its structure; this was a major preoccupation of the workshop's participants. It was indeed agreed that structural violence such as that which has been perpetuated by the whites was a war of sorts against the non-whites in South Africa. Many non-whites were and remain committed to a negotiated peaceful change. Some have turned to the use of violence. The optimal strategies for change were among the major issues discussed by the workshop. While violence, both direct and structural, is likely to continue, the workshops nonetheless considered how negotiations could be advanced whenever and wherever opportunities arise.

Our second major concern was the decolonization of Namibia. South Africa continues to hold the territory, not only against the will of the Namibians, but also the entire world. There are two paths to independence in Namibia. One is through intensified fighting and the other through mediation. It is apparent that a new mediation effort is required. The workshop focused on likely avenues for third parties, although most participants saw little reason for hope in the light of South African intransigence and bad faith.

Our last issue for discussion was peace, security and development in the entire region of Southern Africa. There is an obvious link between what happens inside South Africa and the pace of the movement towards Namibian independence on the one hand, and the military and economic situation in the region, on the other.

The IPA, from its inception, has been actively engaged in peaceful change and the negotiated resolution of conflicts. Other individuals, countries and liberation movements have to make their own choices. We at the Academy are fully aware of the limits to negotiations, in particular that certain situations have to get worse before parties agree to go to the bargaining table. But sooner or later they must, and even South Africa is no exception. In this context, we are committed to leave no opportunity for negotiation unexplored. That is, we seek to get parties to the table sooner rather than later.

The IPA has a total commitment to the rights of man and civil liberties. When these are violated, the Academy will make itself available to offer assistance, with its limited resources and within the framework of our mandate of being a training and research institute for peacemaking, peacekeeping and peacebuilding. The major endeavors of the Academy have been devoted to the preparation of leadership. Its network of alumni and resource persons involved in the Academy's activities makes communications possible between a variety of people who are deemed essential prerequisites in the search for peaceful solutions.

New York   Indar Jit Rikhye
May 1986

ACKNOWLEDGEMENTS

The Second International Conference of Peace and Security in Southern Africa was held in Dar es Salaam in collaboration with the Ministry of Foreign Affair's Centre for Foreign Relations and the University of Dar es Salaam, March 2—6, 1986. The International Peace Academy is indebted to the Centre for making available the facilities at the Arusha International Conference Centre, and we are grateful for the splendid cooperation of the Centre's staff. In particular, I would like to thank my co-chairmen of the workshop: Mr. Anthony M. Hokororo, Director of the Centre for Foreign Relations, and Mr. Nicholas Kuhanga, Vice Chancellor of the University of Dar es Salaam. Especially commendable is the important contribution to the organization of the conference made by Dr. Ibrahim Msabaha, the Centre's Director of Studies and Programmes, and by Dr. Thomas G. Weiss, Executive Director of the Academy, who were most ably assisted by Mr. Hamisi Kibola of the Centre and Miss Charlotte House of the Academy in coordinating the administrative arrangements. My thanks also go to Dr. Ali Khalif Galaydh, Research Fellow at the Centre for Middle Eastern Studies, Harvard University, who served as an IPA consultant, and to all those on the staffs of the Centre and the Academy who so ably helped in making this meeting a success.

The discussions were skillfully summarized by H.E. Mr. Ilkka Ristimaki, Ambassador of Findland to the United Republic of Tanzania, who served as rapporteur; it was an honor to have had the insights from someone who knows so well the political and economic complexities of this troubled region. Contributing to the substantive issues of the conference were background papers prepared by an eclectic group of resource staff, of which most have been reproduced in this report.

Lastly, the conference would not have been possible without the financial assistance of the Ford and Rockefeller Foundations. Our special thanks are extended to Mrs. Enid Schoettle of the Ford Foundation and Mr. John Stremlau of the Rockefeller Foundation for their vision and interest in supporting these activities.

New York   Indar Jit Rikhye
April 1986

Southern Africa

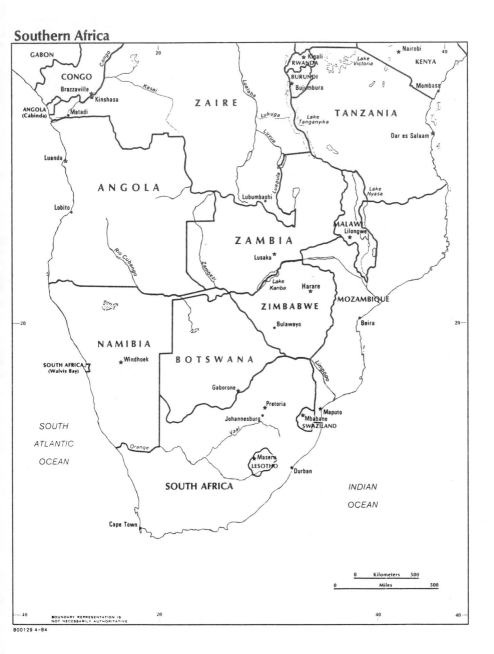

The boundaries and names shown on this map do not imply official endorsement or acceptance by the International Peace Academy.

CONCLUSIONS

The Second International Conference on Peace and Security in Southern Africa met at the International Conference Centre in Arusha, United Republic of Tanzania, 2–6 March, 1986. This meeting was sponsored and organized by the Centre for Foreign Relations and the University of Dar es Salaam and by the International Peace Academy, New York. The meeting was attended by 96 participants and observers, including officials of some 26 countries, three liberation movements, and the OAU as well as practitioners and opinion-makers.

The conference was inaugurated by the Hon. Joseph Sinde Warioba MP, Prime Minister and First Vice-President of the United Republic of Tanzania. The meeting was presided over by three co-chairmen: Mr. Anthony M. Hokororo, Director of the Centre for Foreign Relations; Mr. Nicholas Kuhanga, Vice Chancellor of the University of Dar es Salaam; and Major General Indar Jit Rikhye (Retd), President of the International Peace Academy. H.E. Mr. Ilkka Ristimaki, Ambassador of Finland in Dar es Salaam, acted as Rapporteur.

The first order of business was the approval of a message of condolence to Mrs. Olof Palme and family as well as the government and the people of Sweden following the tragic and senseless death of the Prime Minister.

The working sessions took place as an informal and off-the-record workshop. Participants acted in their personal capacities in order to get beyond the rigidities of official positions and to explore the complexities of political, military, economic and social developments in the region with a view to enhancing the prospects for peaceful social change in the sub-region.

On the last day, the participants sought consensus on conclusions that the group as a whole could support. A draft was submitted and further modified. The paragraphs below represent the consensus that emerged from that process.

The conclusions of the Second International Conference on Peace and Security in Southern Africa are:

The frontline states' search for security

1. The root cause of violence in the region is apartheid and the main purpose behind the Republic of South Africa's (RSA) military and economic actions is the preservation of white minority rule. In addition to the need to satisfy domestic public opinion, military activities are directed towards achieving significant leverage over the behaviour of neighboring countries: and in some cases the actual objective is more far-reaching, namely the change in the governments of the frontline states (FLS).

2. The military predominance of the RSA is obvious. However, its effectiveness over time in terms of invading neighboring states is not necessarily the same for its use internally as a repressive force.

3. Although their military position is undoubtedly weak in comparison with that of the RSA, the FLS and their leaders have nonetheless been responsible for significant political achievements in recent years on Zimbabwe and Namibia in negotiations with Western powers. Further explorations of their potential role as third-parties, particularly in light of the Commonwealth team's efforts, is certainly merited if opportunities for creative mediation are not to be missed.

4. There is an unequivocal preference for peaceful solutions to the region's problems, yet the present is unpropitious for negotiations. In the light of failures in the Nkomati and Lusaka agreements, the good faith of the RSA is seriously in question. The impossibility of meaningful negotiations while apartheid remains is a reality; once dismantled, there would be more room

to negotiate. In the meanwhile, opportunities to influence the negotiating environment should be fully explored.

5. The FLS have always sought peace and never military confrontation with the RSA, and regret the paradox of an increasing need to resort to armed struggle in order to advance the cause of peace. Sanctions are the main non-military option supported by them and much of the international community, to exert pressure on the RSA to force the end of apartheid. Over time, sanctions and disinvestment have become increasingly acceptable policy options that can influence policies and attitudes within the RSA. Its black majority and the neighboring countries are prepared to make the sacrifice entailed, but they clearly would require massive international assistance to compensate for economic losses and withstand likely RSA reprisals. There is a link between responses by the international community and the struggle within the RSA, the former being insufficient to bring the RSA to the bargaining table. Internal pressures are essential in order to make international responses more effective. In order to have the largest impact, sanctions must be universal — including all countries not only from the West but also the East and South — although a concentration on selected products and a phase approach to escalating steps might also lead to results. The main trading partners of the RSA should be persuaded that their own long-run economic and strategic interests would be best served by majority rule in all of Southern Africa.

6. The RSA has achieved economic hegemony and uses it to create dependency and destabilization in neighboring countries. The individual collective economic weaknesses of the FLS result in a situation in which they have little leverage to resist destabilization efforts. To the extent that there are ethnic controversies and unbalanced economic growth, there will be potential conflicts that can be manipulated.

7. The main effort of the FLS themselves to reduce dependency on the RSA and to promote integrated regional development has been the Southern African Development Coordination Committee (SADCC). Weak economies and destabilization efforts will inhibit

regional economic cooperation and development. While SADCC has been largely successful in coordinating development financing and in attracting financial resources, the implementation of regional development plans has made little progress. The SADCC route, by its nature, will show results only in a medium to longer term; it should nonetheless be given strong support. In additon to efforts by these countries themselves, increased support by the international community for SADCC and the Preferential Trade Agreement (PTA) is essential. Regional efforts would continue to be necessary even after majority rule is established in all of Southern Africa.

Namibian independence[1]

8. The RSA appeared willing to accept independence for Namibia, but not under SWAPO leadership. Therefore it has long postponed the implementation of Security Council Resolution 435 and free elections. The likely SWAPO victory in elections would be equated with victory for the practice of armed struggle and such a victory was a precedent that the RSA could not afford. At the same time, independence without SWAPO would not receive international recognition, and therefore was not viable. The RSA has therefore tried to defeat SWAPO militarily, strengthen the Multi-Party Conference (MPC) parties and by-pass Resolution 435 by reaching an agreement bilaterally with SWAPO.

9. The linkage to the withdrawal of Cuban troops from Angola is a convenience to postpone independence. Even if the linkage issue were resolved, it is likely that the RSA would seize upon still another pretext to prevent implementation of Resolution 435.

10. SWAPO's policy is to continue the armed struggle in the extremely difficult conditions prevailing in Namibia in order to apply the pressure necessary to bring the RSA to the negotiating

[1]An announcement was made by President Botha on Namibian independence on 4 March, the very day the workshop itself discussed this issue. It was noted that nothing in the speech changed the conclusions.

table. No quick breakthrough is expected. Internally, an erosion is taking place among the MPC parties, some of which are aligning themselves with SWAPO.

11. In addition to the intransigence of the RSA, the present impasse is seen as largely due to the reluctance of the United States to extend its influence in favor of Namibian independence — in particular, its insistence on linking independence to the issue of Cuban troops as well as its support of UNITA. Thus, whatever means available — diplomatic, the media, interventions by public figures, activities by non-governmental organizations — should be employed to help alter US public opinion on this matter.

12. The prospects for third party roles in relation to independence for Namibia — by the UN, by the FLS, by the Contact Group or individual members of it, and by the Commonwealth team — are not bright. Nonetheless, every negotiating opportunity should be seized.

Inside South Africa

13. While the structures of white supremacy are still intact, a significant change in the balance of internal forces has occurred in comparison with the situation prevailing when the 1948 legislation on apartheid was enacted. Instead of being arrogant, the white minority is now on the defensive; they are concerned with how much power to surrender in order to keep as much power as possible and even to insure their own future. There is a widespread recognition that the 300 year-old system of white minority rule cannot continue, and evidence is emerging of its gradual disintegration. Rather than reform, these developments can be described as containing the seeds of a revolutionary process. Whether this process leads to fundamental changes without an all-engulfing outbreak of violence remains to be seen.

14. A peaceful solution to conflicts has always been the first choice of the OAU. Only when it became evident that this approach was not possible did liberation movements resort to the

use of armed struggle as means to promote negotiations. The choices before the RSA are thus: negotiations with representative leaders from all groups about majority rule; or entrenchment and repression as a prelude to increasing violence and civil war.

15. The fundamental task of those interested in negotiation is to strengthen the forces that make negotiations possible and counter the opposing forces. There is thus an essential and growing role for the churches, the media, corporate investors and labor unions — both in the RSA and elsewhere — in urging the release of all political prisoners and the return of all exiles as well as the unbanning of all congress movements; calling for the imposition of such non-violent means as sanctions and divestment to bring pressure to bear on the RSA; and seeking to define a negotiating agenda.

16. Since the early 1960s, liberation movements have relied upon armed struggle as the means to resist oppression and to secure self-liberation. In their assessment, without the armed capability of confronting the RSA and making it ungovernable, victory over apartheid is not possible.

17. The RSA must be judged on its actions and not its words. Liberation movements should not be called upon to negotiate when negotiations are diversionary from the point of view of the overall struggle. No opportunity exists for fruitful negotiations at this juncture. Existing contacts can be strengthened and new channels of communication opened among the various parties involved. The process leading to meaningful negotiations may be long and require pressure against the RSA by various means available, including armed struggle as well as mass civil action and activities by the trade unions, churches, mass media and other organizations. When this pressure has created opportune conditions for negotiations, then communications channels established may prove to be of considerable value. While there is skepticism about the success of efforts such as those of the Commonwealth team, there is nonetheless a need not to overlook any possible opening. As a minimum the issues should be constantly kept alive before the public.

Leadership and the future

18. Skills building is required for the future generation of South African and Namibian leaders. Among other things, both during the immediate future as well as after democratic rule has been established, professionals are required who can manage internal and external communications, build alliances, and know when and how to negotiate. The International Peace Academy is an independent, non-governmental organization that can help build such professional skills and should do so for future leaders of South Africa and Namibia as well as of the FLS. The IPA has been able to bring together an unusually diverse group of practitioners, analysts and opinion-makers to discuss peace and security in Southern Africa; the IPA is encouraged to organize another such workshop in 1987.

SUMMARY OF DISCUSSIONS

Ali Khalif Galaydh
Research Fellow, Center for Middle Eastern Studies,
Harvard University

Part I: The format and the agenda

The Second International Conference on Peace and Security in Southern Africa (March 2–6, 1986) included three days of working sessions to stimulate wide-ranging discussions among the participants. Nine papers (see pages 9–174) were commissioned by the International Peace Academy from individuals with a wide range of governmental, international and academic experience. The agenda for the conference included:

a) Opening address
b) Military security in the region
c) Economic security in the region
d) Mediation in Namibia
e) Inside South Africa
f) Leadership and the future
g) Conclusions

Part II: Principal themes in the discussion

Theme I: The frontline states' search for security

The security of the FLS is very much part of the liberation of

Namibia and of dismantling apartheid. The termination of the illegal occupation of Namibia and the abolishing of apartheid are not only just causes but also non-negotiable. The current correlation of force favors the Republic of South Africa. The quality of its military hardware (though aging in some areas) and the training and morale of its defense forces afford the Republic a disproportionate advantage vis-à-vis the armed forces of its neighbors. The command, control and communication systems of the SADF have no equal on the continent. Their intelligence gathering and analysis is superior, even by international standards.

The military objectives of the RSA in the sub-region and the search for security in the neighboring states were examined in light of the primary goal: the prservation of white minority rule in the Republic. Pre-empting support for liberation movements in neighboring countries is also another significant objective. While these were seen by the participants to be defensive policy positions, there are also offensive policy instruments. A primary policy instrument, especially since the ascension of P.W. Botha to power and the related development of the State Security Council into a dominant force in the decision-making processes, has been the destabilization of the neighboring states. Economic destruction and the delegitimization (even engineering the overthrow of unfriendly governments) of uncooperative neighboring states are conscious policy instrument for enhancing or at least maintaining the critical security leverage which the Republic possesses in the sub-region.

The policy options available to the FLS in their search for security appear to be narrow. The internal conflicts in some of them, such as Angola, provide South Africa with convenient entry points to intervene. Entering into non-aggression pacts with South Africa appears ineffective to bring about peace. The Nkomati Accord has portrayed the inability or unwillingness of the South African government to deliver its part of security deals. The bilateral military cooperation between Mozambique and Zimbabwe has led to instances of success in combatting RENAMO and ensuring the safety of the oil pipeline to the Zimbabwe refinery.

The relative military weakness of the FLS has not barred them from effective dipolmatic negotiations for the independence of

Zimbabwe and the unanimous passing of Security Council Resolution 435. The peaceful resolution of the internal South Africa conflict and the liberation of Namibia are far from being attainable in the near future. The state of violence in South Africa during the last eighteen months and the subsequent declaration of emergency have exposed the internal weakness of the Republic. The police are unable to cope with law and order and the SADF are increasingly deployed in the black townships. The independence of Namibia is entangled in the Angolan internal conflict which in turn has evolved into an East-West issue. The support of UNITA by the Reagan administration has further weakened prospects for negotiated settlement in Angola, Namibia and perhaps the whole sub-region. There are presently no mechanisms to replace the Contact Group; and the cooperation between the FLS and the major Western countries, which was instrumental for the independence of Zimbabwe, is not obtaining. Armed struggle by the liberation movements and destabilization by the SADF are emerging as the significant policy choices.

The international community has a responsibility to promote a peaceful resolution to the multiple conflicts in the sub-region, particularly the core conflict in South Africa itself. The conditions do not appear to be auspicious at the moment, but the need is felt for international initiatives based on the realities of the area. In the meantime, the FLS individually, bilaterally or as a group have to design appropriate strategies for meeting the security needs of their peoples.

Theme II: Peace and economic security considerations in the region

The economies of the Southern African states are in a serious crisis. Their post-independence economic performance has not been impressive, particularly in the area of food production and agriculture. The food security requirements of these countries are not being met, partly because of the economic development strategies they have pursued; inclement weather conditions in the region; and also the destabilization policies of the government of South Africa, which results in the destruction of the basic infrastructure and diversion of economic resources to military/ security needs.

Destabilization by South Africa takes advantage of the internal conflicts of the countries of the region as convenient entry points. What destabilization does is to preempt the development of viable options for the FLS in terms of transport, regional economic cooperation, and development.

The response of the majority-ruled countries of the region has been the creation of institutions like the Preferential Trade Agreement (PTA), but more particularly the Southern African Development Coordination Conference (SADCC). The purpose of SADCC is the reduction of dependence on South Africa, the promotion of regional integration and also, with a view to the fact that economic cooperation cannot be isolated from security considerations, the provison of a regional security umbrella.

With regard to the question of economic sanctions against the regime in South Africa, a consensus emerged that the issue is not whether to apply sanctions, but what type would be most effective in bringing South Africa to the negotiating table and what the costs will be involved for the various parties. But, in evaluating this last aspect, what must be taken into account is the lack of other options available to accomplish this purpose.

The application of sanctions must take into consideration the objectives to be achieved; maximizing the cost to South Africa while minimizing the impact to the FLS; and the particular vulnerabilities of the South African economy, which lie primarily in the areas of exports and foreign investment.

Sanctions by themselves will not bring about a significant policy change, but can complement such developments inside the Republic of South Africa as urban violence, consumer and school boycotts, strikes and work stoppages by the trade unions, which have exposed the internal weaknesses of the apartheid regime. Sanctions must be applied in conjunction with the internal liberation struggle, be that armed or non-violent.

In addition, the timing and phasing of sanctions should be so designed as to bring about a dismantling of apartheid, while preventing the necessary adjustments by South Africa in its economy which might neutralize their impact. Finally, in terms of the role of the international community, and particularly of the

OECD countries, the policy options range from support for SADCC (to minimize the costs of destabilization) to the actual application of effective sanctions and support for the liberation movements themselves.

Theme III: Namibian independence

With the passage of Resolution 435, a consensus emerged among the FLS, SWAPO and the Contact Group. The reluctance of South Africa was apparent even then, but the lack of implementation of 435 was related to the internal conflict in Angola, which has been internationalized in the interim.

There has been no significant profess since 1979. The SADF have the upper hand, although not without significant costs. SWAPO has maintained its positions against the internal settlement forces, although it has been less visible in recent years.

South Africa will attempt to retain Namibia by all available means. A SWAPO victory in an election process would be a confirmation of the role of armed liberation struggle. It would establish a precedent for the internal politics of South Africa itself. A SWAPO victory would be perceived as enhancing the position of the Soviet Union and its allies in the region. In terms of South African security considerations, there are those who favor a buffer zone in Namibia, arguing that the line along the Cunene River is more defensible than one along the Orange River. Finally, there are extensive vested economic interests in Namibia, particularly of the Afrikaaner community, and in the administration and local politics of Namibia. South Africa could envisage an independent Namibia in the case that their internal settlement mechanism works, i.e., if those in Namibia who are in favor of the dominance of South Africa are put in positions of power.

The linkage issue has provided an opportunity for South Africa that US foreign policy has dictated: the withdrawal of Cuban troops; and a reduction of Soviet influence in Angola and the region. The concept of linkage thus puts South Africa into the strategic framework of the imperatives of US global strategic policy. It provides South Africa with a convenient mechanism to delay the decolonization process and manipulate an internal settlement in Namibia as per their own policy goals.

In terms of the internal ethnic politics of Namibia, SWAPO would have a majority in elections, if held. The complicated balance of ethnic arithmetic is being used to forestall the liberation of Namibia. There is genuine concern on the part of external actors about liberation, justice and the installation of democratic institutions. These issues, however, can be part of the negotiation process, but the imposition of minority rights cannot be pre-conditions for negotiations.

Opportunities and necessary conditions for mediation are not present. South Africa is not yet suffering enough disturbance to induce its genuine participation in such a process, nor are there any international initiatives afoot to pressure South Africa toward the negotiating table. Thus, in all likelihood an increase in the armed struggle will be the likely prelude to a change in South African attitudes.

Theme IV: Inside South Africa: The players and their role in social change

As an overview of the situation inside South Africa, there exists a difference of opinion as to the nature of present political realities. There are those who say that some meaningful changes are taking place both within the white ruling class and also the extra-parliamentary opposition whose presence is being felt through mass actions. There are divisions within the white ruling class, some of whose members feel that the government has lost its authoritative position and is now governed by manipulation rather than a self-confident, authoritative system. There are also those who see no positive progress, who regard new constitutional dispensation not as a step forward but as one backward because dispossession and denationalization are still being carried out.

There are also differnces of perception of the prospects for fundamental change between those who perceive the possibility for such change and those who see a continuation of the apartheid system under another guise.

There are also differences of perception of the prospects for through an acceleration of such measures as the cooperation of the homeland leaders; and fundamental change in which the power structure is totally transformed to majority rule.

The main actors in the present or future development of South Africa are the church, the business community, the trade unions, the media and the liberation movements.

Churches

The Dutch Reform Church has provided apartheid with a legitimizing ideology. There are, however, serious divisions within the church and it is very much isolated from the mainstream Christian churches. The militant position of the churches is not merely theological. On the contrary, the broader, social and political issues of liberation and justice are their focus. The question is no longer the issue of violence or non-violence, because of the structural violence perpetuated by the apartheid system.

Media

The mass media is very much under the control of South African authorities; as in many African countries, it is not free. The anti-apartheid struggle has no access to the establishment media and must therefore resort to ad hoc community based media. Image manipulation by the South African authorities is graphically portrayed by black on black violence. The attempted manipulation of the mass media and the agonizing realities of South Africa have led to the polarization of correspondents of the international commercial media in South Africa. This manipulation serves three purposes: a) control of the flow of information to supporters (power-base) and purported enemies, where the image conveyed of the liberation movements is one of terrorists; b) denial of access of media channels to the anti-apartheid struggle; and c) control of the flow of television pictures of rioting and violence abroad, which was having a significant impact on international public opinion.

Corporate investors

The recent developments in South Africa have created a crisis of confidence for both the domestic business community and for foreign investors. The business community is perceived to be part of the existing socio-economic and political system. Corporate investors have attempted to distance themselves from the government. The business community can play a positive role in grappling with the issues of equitable distribution of resources and thereby improve their credibility with the black community. It can play a role in facilitating negotiations, but can hardly be expected to engage in bringing about systemic change.

Labor unions

The labor union movement, especially since 1973, has been in the forefront of the demand for change. There seems to be a division of opinion as to whether the black trade unions should focus on such work-related issues as unfair labor practices or deal with broader political and social issues. The relative freedom of trade unionism is still constrained by instruments such as influx control which effectively bans freedom to strike. The formation of a 'Congress of South African Trade Unions' (COSATU) in December 1985 has provided the movement with a strong bargaining position. The innovative, decentralized and democratic structures of the trade unions have facilitated the outflanking of banning and detention practices by authorities. The effectiveness of trade unions will be based on their handling of purely economic-union issues and their collaboration with mass-based organizations.

Liberation movements

Fundamental change in South Africa can hardly be brought about unless sufficient pressure is applied against the apartheid system. Fundamental change will require a counterpoint to the total strategy and dominant power position of the ruling white elite. The liberation movements have been forced to resort to armed struggle since 1960, after the failure of non-violent means. There is no viable substitute for effective armed struggle at the present time. Armed struggle and other appropriate strategies have to be based on the concrete conditions in South Africa. There was concern in the discussion for a closing of the ranks of the various liberation movements in order to ensure maximum impact and to thwart the divide-and-rule precepts of the apartheid system.

Theme V: Leadership and the future

The present conditions are not auspicious for mediation and negotiation. But securing lines of communication and building bridges will prove to be useful when conditions are ripe. The future generation of South African and Namibian leaders require professional training in crisis management. The International Peace Academy can assist in this process by preparing professionals in the skills of peacekeeping, peacemaking and peacebuilding.

COMPILATION OF PAPERS

Opening Statement by the Prime Minister and First Vice-President, Ndugu Joseph S. Warioba, at the International Conference on Peace and Security in Southern Africa, AICC, Arusha 3rd March, 1986

Mr. Chairman,
Distinguished Participants,
Ladies and Gentlemen.

It is an honor for me, on behalf of the Government, and people of Tanzania, to welcome such a group of eminent personalities to Arusha and Tanzania to discuss a subject which is important to the entire world and so close to our hearts in this sub-region. I hope the people of Arusha, on behalf of Tanzania, will make your stay comfortable and the leadership and staff of the Arusha International Conference Centre will provide you with the necessary facilities to make your deliberations fruitful.

I would like to thank the Centre for Foreign Relations, the University of Dar es Salaam and the Peace Academy for inviting me to open this conference on Peace and Security in Southern Africa. I would also like to pay particular tribute to the International Peace Academy and Major General Indar Jit Rikhye for the interest and practical support which they have shown in organizing this conference. Over the years, the International Peace Academy has earned itself a distinguished record in conducting training packages in dispute settlement and conflict management, and also in conducting research in issues of regional security. I welcome the Academy to Tanzania and commend its work in the interests of our region.

In this regard, I am confident that the training seminar on negotiation, co-sponsored by the Academy and the Centre for Foreign Relations, which preceded this Conference last week, has contributed to a greater understanding by the participants of the processes involved in negotiation and dispute settlement.

The issues of peace and security in Southern Africa still dominate the agenda of regional discussions in our sub-region. Inside South Africa, events have taken such a catastrophic turn that something rapidly approaching a civil war is in the making. The apartheid regime, having proclaimed a state of emergency in a great number of the African townships, has had to deploy the army in these areas because the police are no longer able to cope with the problems of law and order. Even then, as events show, its grip on the situation is becoming increasingly precarious. In a period of twelve months, more than one thousand people have died in the unrest as victims of the repressive security forces of the apartheid regime. Despite this obvious drift to catastrophe, there is yet no indication that the regime is ready to dismantle the inhuman system of apartheid. Instead, it has unleashed a reign of terror both against its population and against its neighbors. It also continues to occupy Namibia illegally, and uses it for launching attacks against the Republic of Angola.

There is no doubt in our mind that apartheid is the source of all the violence and injustice and instability in Southern Africa.

The prime motive of South Africa's deep-rooted opposition to genuine independence for Namibia is the defense of apartheid. Similarly, the paramount motive for South Africa's aggression and subversive attacks against free African States is the defense of apartheid. South Africa is afraid of the example of independent African States committed to the principles of justice and human equality. It is also clear to us that the defense of apartheid is the purpose of the South African regime's killings, its torture, bannings, and its detentions of South African citizens.

There are three main elements which I would like to emphasise in a discussion of the political situation in Southern Africa. First is the issue of the independence of Namibia.

Security Council Resolution 435 was adopted unanimously in 1978. In theory, the United Nations Plan for the Independence of Namibia has been agreed by all those who are directly involved in the details of this question. These include SWAPO, the South African Government, the members of the Western Contact Group, and the frontline states. Yet Namibia still languishes under colonialism.

Worse still, South Africa is able to remain confident in its defiance of world opinion and the United Nations of the independence of Namibia. Very often we see that resolutions passed on the independence of Namibia are not matched by practical steps of implementation.

This in turn encourages the South African regime to believe that it will not suffer either economically or politically because of its defiance. South Africa's confidence is bolstered by the knowledge that while it serves its own interests of continuing to colonize Namibia it also acts on behalf of the United States of America.

As the history of the negotiations concerning the independence of Namibia show, the linkage between Namibian independence under Resolution 435 and the withdrawal of Cuban troops from Angola was not put forward until sometime after the so-called 'Pre-Implementation Talks' in Geneva in 1981. It was only submitted as a condition for implementing the resolution after the 'linkage' had been made by the present United States Administration during the Presidential campaign in that country at that time. Moreover, all other obstacles in the way of Resolution 435 raised by South Africa had been overcome. Linkage has thus been doubly serving the interests of South Africa. Apart from creating an obstacle to the independence of Namibia, linkage has provided the excuse for the South African regime to continue destabilizing Angola and thus make it impossible for Angola to agree to the withdrawal of Cuban troops. In turn, this ensures continued American support for South Africa's defiance of the United Nations. The open support and massive material assistance by South Africa and the United States to Savimbi and his terrorist organization UNITA, is a clear testimony to this.

The purpose of Resolution 435 was to effect a peaceful transfer of power to the Namibian people and thereby avoid the misery and suffering of a protracted armed struggle for independence.

Resolution 435 was an attempt to fulfil one of the functions for which the United Nations was established, that is, the prevention of war and the settlement of conflict by peaceful means. After eight years of non-implementation of Resolution 435, the question to ask is not only whether this peaceful alternative to the independence of Namibia is viable, but for how long and in the face of how much South African and American obstruction Africa and the international community will continue to regard it as an alternative. The people of Namibia, under the leadership of SWAPO, the frontline states, Africa and the entire world, have waited with patience since the Western Contact Group took some initiatives which led to the adoption of Resolution 435. We have waited patiently, even when the Contact Group ceased to pursue an active and meaningful role in the search for a peaceful solution in Namibia. We have waited with patience and trust to see the outcome of the consultations undertaken by the United States. It is with dismay that we now note that the emphasis in the consultations has been diverted from the central issue, which is the independence of Namibia, to issues which are alien to Namibian and African purposes.

What I am saying is that the failure of negotiated peaceful settlement in Namibia does not leave any other choice to the people of Namibia under SWAPO except to intensify the armed struggle for their liberation. In fact, the potential of Africa and the international community to assist the liberation struggle in Namibia grew out of the resounding victories of FRELIMO in Mozambique, MPLA in Angola and ZANU in Zimbabwe. It was these developments which had the effect of strengthening the international consensus on Namibia, finally leading to Resolution 435.

The alternative of armed struggle is applicable also to the situation inside South Africa, which constitutes what I would like to take as the second element in the political situation in Southern Africa.

Historically, the liberation movements in South Africa were established as pacifist movements, conducting peaceful protests and passive resistance as ways of effecting change in South Africa.

Successive Southern African Governments, however, have consistently responded by violence, repression and an intensification of racial oppression. The repression and violence takes the form of arbitrary imprisonment, torture, violent deaths in prison, indiscriminate killings of innocent and unarmed people by the security agents of the apartheid regime. The mass murders of opponents of apartheid at Sharpeville, Langa and Soweto are still vivid in our memories. These systematic brutal murders can be likened to the Nazi atrocities of the 1940s, the only difference being that the apartheid killings are mini-holocausts. And the apartheid authorities had clamped a ban on reports on its violence in the vain hope that the world will stay ignorant of what is happening.

The violence of apartheid has forced the freedom movements to organize their activities for freedom and defense as an armed struggle. In recent years, the internal resistance to apartheid has grown stronger, more widespread, more open and more desperate. It is also spontaneous. No-one, no organization and no country outside South Africa, including the independent neighboring states, could instigate it or stop it. Therefore, to explain this phenomenon of resistance in South Africa as the result of instigation by neighbors and outsiders who give support to so-called terrorists is to lie blatantly. Such lies reflect a siege mentality which the internal resistance has wrought on the South African regime. The regime would like the world to believe that if there were no mischievous neighbors there would be no ANC, and if there were no ANC there would be no internal Black resistance!

The African townships, notwithstanding the permanent presence of the army, are now for the most part effectively off limits to the regime. Within most of these townships, the structures of local administration imposed by the regime have disintegrated. It is also noteworthy that the apartheid regime is now finding it practically impossible to recruit new collaborators to run its discredited local institutions. Life in the townships cannot be described in any meaningful sense as normal.

How should the international community respond to the looming catastrophe in South Africa? We believe that the crisis in South Africa calls for seriousness and determination in working for the dismantling of apartheid. It is therefore doubly immoral for outsiders to stand in the way of the efforts of the people of South Africa to free themselves from the oppression and the violence of the immoral system of apartheid.

Africa and the frontline states recognise that the violence inherent in apartheid does not lend itself to political dialogue. Consequently, negotiations concerning the future of South Africa cannot take place within the framework of the political dominance of apartheid. The essence of apartheid, which is white minority monopoly of political and economic power, and control of the black majority, must first be removed before a realistic dialogue can take place amongst the genuine representatives of the different racial groups in South Africa.

It is therefore important to be aware of the attempts of the South African Government to deceive outsiders by proclaiming that it is willing to reform apartheid. South African propaganda relies heavily on world ignorance of the details of apartheid. Desegragating park benches, restaurants, and repeal of the Immorality Act, for example, mean very little in comparison to the disfranchisement of all indigenous black Africans, which essentially is the cornerstone or apartheid. None of the reforms announced by the Botha administration has any significant meaning, and none has been intended to have a meaning.

The United Nations has declared apartheid as a crime against humanity. The moral and legal basis of apartheid is an affront to humanity. It is therefore the moral obligation of humanity to seek the total destruction of this obnoxious system.

The international community can contribute to the fight against apartheid through the application of both mandatory and comprehensive sanctions on South Africa. Sanctions are necessary to force a peaceful change. It is the only viable peaceful solution left, and change must be induced if we are to avoid a total conflagration in South Africa. Contrary to the now familiar excuses, sanctions do work. South Africa itself has shown how effective sanctions can be by blockading Lesotho and boycotting Maputo Port. In any case, the undoubted cost of major sanctions to black South Africans and to neighboring states has to be balanced against the higher cost to them of the present system of apartheid.

My third and final point relates to the relations between South Africa and its neighbors. In his speech to Parliament on 31st January, 1986, President P.W. Botha declared:

> 'I again stretch out the hand of friendship to our neighbors. Let us reach an agreement on the specific rules of the game regulating the conduct of neighbors towards one another. . . . Should this invitation by the Republic of South Africa be ignored or rejected, we have no other choice but to take effective steps to protect our country and population against threats.'

Botha's outstretched hand of friendship to South Africa's neighbors is an arrogant and veiled threat. He is threatening his neighbors that if they don't acquiesce in the domination of apartheid, they will be punished. The violence and terrorism of apartheid spills over into neighboring countries. The South African Government has searched and attacked the liberation movements in neighboring states and in the process killed indiscriminately. It has done this in Mozambique, in Lesotho, in Botswana, in Angola, in Zimbabwe and in Swaziland.

The purpose of South Africa's attacks, whether directly or through indirect aggression, is to destabilize the states on its borders and the borders of Namibia. The price for immunity from South African military attacks and organized subversion is that the neighboring states should give up their independence and act as South Africa's policemen, arresting and expelling members of the South African Liberation Movements on its behalf.

Mr. Chairman, this Conference is being attended by participants of a high calibre, who are well informed about the issues of peace and security in Southern Africa. Indeed, the obstacle to the solution of the political problems confronting us in this region is not lack of information on what is happening. It is a result of the contradictions that impede a will to act decisively. I am confident that the scholarship, the expertise and the experience of the delegates to this conference will generate a useful exchange and perhaps provide fresh insights into how best and quickly to solve the problems of apartheid and colonialism in South Africa.

I would like to reiterate that as far as Tanzania is concerned there is no question of our lessening continued support for the just struggle of the people of Namibia and South Africa.

I wish you very stimulating and fruitful deliberations and a pleasant stay in Arusha and in our country.

Thank you.

THE FRONTLINE STATES' SEARCH FOR SECURITY*

Kurt M. Campbell
Center for Science and International Affairs, Kennedy School of
Government, Harvard University

10 May 1986

The recent spate of domestic upheaval in South Africa has spurred
a renewed optimism in the West and among Southern Africa's
frontline states that a fundamental reorientation from white
minority to black majority rule may be near at hand. While 1984
witnessed a number of successful South African domestic and
international initiatives, these fleeting gains vanished during 1985
in the face of mounting black rage and defiance. The black townships have become all but ungovernable, and State President
P.W. Botha declared a state of emergency and deployed the army
in many areas of the country in attempts to quell the unrest.
The international community has reacted with concern to South
Africa's turmoil, and the disinvestment campaign continues to
gain momentum in government, academic and commercial circles
in the United States. Many Western banks called in their loans to
South Africa and President Reagan himself, formerly an ardent
supporter of the Republic, instituted limited economic sanctions
against the white regime.

Yet, while there are clear signs of trouble for the white leaders
of Afrikanerdom. the regime is much more stable and entrenched
than popularly believed. Indeed, the political, economic and

---

*An earlier version of this essay was delivered to the Second International Conference
on Peace and Security in Southern Africa held in Arusha, Tanzania, between 2—6 March,
1986, and sponsored by the International Peace Academy of New York.

particularly military power available to Pretoria is largely intact and consequently there is little prospect in the immediate future of a transformation from white to black power. It can be said that apartheid's strategists have lost their grand strategy for managing South Africa's racial problems, and with it their confidence and optimism for the future, but Pretoria remains convinced of its capability to deal militarily with any domestic, and for that matter, regional contingency. The black opposition within South Africa is divided and severely constrained by the security apparatus. The ANC has been generally successful in winning over the hearts and minds of many black South Africans and in establishing international prestige, but the fighting wing of the organization, *Unkonto We Sizwe*, has fared poorly when matched against the state. Much of the urban turmoil in South Africa has occurred spontaneously and not as a result of an ANC orchestrated campaign. The ANC's leadership in exile was, from many accounts, caught off-guard by the suddenness and ferocity of the fighting in South Africa and has had to struggle to keep abreast of the situation.

Since the crescendo of public awareness over South Africa in the spring of 1985, the government has tried desperately to stem the torrent of domestic disturbance and blunt international criticism. Some of these efforts have failed, such as the bungling public diplomacy between Foreign Minister Pik Botha and former United States National Security Council adviser Bud McFarlane, and State President Botha's much heralded but ultimately disappointing 'Rubicon' speech. Yet, a number of Pretoria's actions have brought the government some badly needed time and space to maneuver. The South Africans correctly determined the correlation between Western outrage and the pictures of urban rioting appearing on nightly television newscasts. The government moved swiftly to terminate any camera reporting of violence after accusing the Western media of staging several events. Pretoria initially also renounced some of the major insignificant statutes of apartheid legislation such as the Mixed Marriages Act, but when these gestures failed to satisfy South Africa's critics, the government in April 1986 abolished the so-called Pass Laws, long regarded as the basis of the entire strategy of separate development.

In addition to these domestic measures, Pretoria has generally attempted to keep a lower international profile.

Although investor confidence in South Africa's future has been shattered, some of the wind in the anti-apartheid movement's sails has died, at least for the time being. South Africa's domestic environment continues to seethe with discord and oppression, but the sense of urgency to wrest power from the white authorities has declined. Western attention refocused on the state of super-power relations during the autumn Reagan-Gorbachev summit (and more recently, terrorism, the confrontation between the US and Libya, and the Chernobyl nuclear disaster have drawn attention away from South Africa), and since, the subject of debate in Southern Africa has centered around Angola and Dr. Jonas Savimbi's UNITA movement. What to do about communism in Southern Africa, rather than apartheid, currently tops the American political agenda. In any case, both supporters and opponents of South Africa are coming to realize that the government's position is more secure and the prospects for fundamental change are more daunting than previously imagined.

What has perhaps gone relatively unnoticed during this period of heightened concern over South Africa's domestic policies, is the increasingly aggressive foreign policy of the Republic towards the frontline states. Indeed, South Africa demonstrated its hegemonic position on the Southern African continent, often clumsily and indiscriminately, to each of its neighbors during 1985. For example, a South African commando team attacked purported quarters of ANC rebels in Gaborone, Botswana. Another South African amphibious team was intercepted by the Angolan authorities during a mission aimed to sabotage the oil producing refineries in the Cabinda Enclave. The joint Zimbabwe-Mozambique military operation against the headquarters of Renamo yielded firm evidence of South Africa's continued support of the anti-government forces, in strict violation of the Nkomati Accord. The South African Defense Force (SADF) stepped up its military support of UNITA during the battles of Menongue, Cuito Cuanavale and Mavinga in southeastern Angola. (The Soviet Union and Cuba also increased their support for the ruling MPLA regime in Angola during 1985.) State President

Botha threatened a 'hot pursuit' of South African forces into Zimbabwe after several ANC landmines detonated in the northernmost Transvaal near the border with Zimbabwe. Finally, the SADF blockaded Lesotho during the recent military coup to oust Prime Minister Jonathan.

In many respects the current phase of South African strategy towards the frontline states is a continuation of traditional policies followed by Pretoria. Since the collapse of the Portuguese African empire in 1975, South Africa has sought to establish and maintain a constellation of compliant regimes to the north. (In many respects, this strategy dates back even further, to Andries Potgieter's drive to lead the *voortrekkers* across the Vaal river against the Ndebele tribe in 1836.) There have been some notable failures for this policy, such as the ill-fated South African intervention into the Angolan civil war, as well as some apparent successes, such as the Nkomati Accord with Mozambique.

The elements of this strategy are essentially fivefold. First, to induce or coerce the frontline states to deny logistical support or refuge for the ANC. Second, to discourage any efforts to relieve reliance on South Africa for economic development or integration, such as the South African Development Coordination Conference (SADCC). Third, to lessen the influence of the USSR and Cuba in Southern Africa. Fourth, to generally weaken the conventional military capabilities of the frontline states. Fifth, since the creation of Zimbabwe following the protracted Rhodesian civil war, the South African government has sought to impede the process of nation building and has generally denigrated the Zimbabwe 'experiment' — thus hoping to deny critics of apartheid an example of a successful transition from white to black power.

Yet in recent months, South Africa's regional strategy appears to have gone beyond creating a 'constellation of states' south of the Cunene-Zambezi. The thrust of South Africa's more recent interventions into neighboring states appears aimed at creating chaos rather than insuring subservience. The new, more aggressive phase of South African policy represents a rejection of US Assistant Secretary of State for African Affairs Chester Crocker's nimble and delicate attempts to coax the Republic away from an indiscriminate involvement in regional destabilization. It marks the ascendance of the military, and particularly the South African

State Security Council in the formulation and execution of foreign policy and the repudiation of diplomacy as a tool of South African statecraft. Indeed, the serious and repeated violations of the Nkomati Accord raises important questions about the ability and willingness of South Africa to adhere to any meaningful or reciprocal agreements with the FLS.

Although this embrace of a more militant approach to relations with the FLS may only be a temporary response to heightened internal discord, this episode should be seen as a warning for the frontline leaders. As international and domestic pressures on the white regime to reform will certainly mount, the military's influence and prestige will also increase commensurately. It is tempting (and ultimately futile) to speculate about what role the military might play in South Africa's domestic evolution, but the signs of the military's capture of foreign policymaking are apparent. Indeed, even a degree of controlled, authoritarian reform at home may usher in a new era of hawkishness abroad. This will doubtless pose serious challenges for the FLS as South Africa's domestic political scene enters a critical phase.

Given the seriousness of South Africa's threat to the stability of the region, what options are available to the frontline leaders in their search for security? The various Southern African states have practiced a number of strategies designed either to deter South African actions or to combat ongoing destabilization. These efforts can be roughly grouped into five categories, principally: pan-African military associations; foreign military assistance; close economic and political relations with the West; nonaggression pacts with South Africa; and ad-hoc regional (bilateral) security arrangements. The degree of effectiveness of each of these measures will be looked at in turn, following a brief review of South Africa's available forms of military and economic power to bring to bear on the region.

South Africa unquestionably possesses the dominant army on the African continent. The Republic has approximately 106,000 persons presently under arms with another 320,000 available reservists. It has an extremely effective air-force which essentially commands the airspace in most of Southern Africa and an efficient coastal navy. After the institution of a United Nations arms embargo against the Republic in the early 1960s, South Africa

established Armscorp, a government sponsored military production corporation. Today, South Africa is virtually self-sufficient
militarily (advanced fighter aircraft is an important exception
here), and exports a variety of superior military hardware to
international clients. Furthermore, South Africa has a useful
communications and intelligence-gathering network and has
traditionally received some assistance from Western intelligence
agencies.

In addition to South Africa's own armed might, Pretoria has
recruited and trained a number of vanquished rebel groups from
the frontline states to the north for use against uncooperative
regimes. Probably the most well-known example are the Renamo
guerrillas, who were sponsored first by Rhodesia and now by
South Africa to create disorder in Mozambique (although South
Africa has provided generous material assistance to Dr Savimbi's
UNITA, the rebel group has also maintained a degree of independence in the formulation of its military strategy and in its
overall political agenda). South Africa has also created the 32nd
battalion of the SADF in Namibia from remnants of the FNLA in
Angola. The army has done much the same with the Angolan
bushmen in the form of the 201 battalion and has provided
sanctuary and training for Bishop Muzorewa's guerrillas from
Zimbabwe and for Lesotho's rebel army in South Africa. Together,
these colonial troops provide a sort of South African foreign
legion which can be unleashed with few domestic or international
repercussions.

South Africa also has a commanding economic and commercial
presence in the surrounding region. In spite of orchestrated calls
from frontline leaders in support of a diplomatic and economic
isolation of the Republic, most of the Southern African economies
are intimately tied to and reliant upon South Africa. For instance,
South Africa's mines host a good number of workers from
surrounding states. South African corporations, such as Anglo-
American and DeBeers, are involved in a vast array of projects
throughout the region. Many of the transportion links and sources
of electric power are managed and controlled by Pretoria. Further,
the South African customs union influences strongly the trade
flow in the region, and indeed neighboring states are becoming
an increasingly important market for South African products.

Thus, taken together, South Africa's political and economic ascendancy assures its predominate position on the continent for the foreseeable future.

The first attempts at Southern African security arrangements are rooted in the formation of the Organization of African Unity (OAU) whose ultimate objective has historically been 'South African liberation'. Indeed, the struggle against apartheid has served as the lowest common denominator and only effective rallying cry for this organization made up of so many diverse nations. Yet, while the OAU in some senses was formed to prosecute a 'holy war' against white rule, it has for much of its history sought to nurture and orchestrate defensive alliances to ward off the superior firepower of Pretoria. Yet the record of the twenty-year long attempts to form some form of pan-African military association — even an African High Command or African Intervention Force — is none too promising. In fact, the call for pan-African military groupings has most often been merely rhetorical, given the overriding problems of organization, expenditure, participation, rivalry, and military strategy. With these obstacles to pan-African military organization on a grand scale, it is probably not a particularly effective vehicle for regional security.

During the so-called 'second-wave' of national liberation which swept Southern Africa in the 1970s, many of the resistance movements looked to international patrons for armed assistance. The former colonial powers, Britain and France, as well as the Western newcomer to African politics, the United States, often opposed these wars and offered little in the way of moral or political support. For the most part, the Soviet Union and China provided the material means to prosecute these struggles for nationhood. China's assistance was most keenly felt during the Rhodesian civil war in their support for Robert Mugabe's ZANU party. However, since 1980, China's involvement in revolutionary politics has declined sharply and the People's Republic is no longer an important factor in Southern African politics. (North Korea and Britain have assisted in the training of Zimbabwe's armed forces, the former with dubious results, and Britain continues to provide some military equipment to Zimbabwe, Zambia and Botswana.) However, the Soviet Union with its allies Cuba and

East Germany have continued to play an active and sometimes vital role in the military affairs of the region.

The socialist community's main contribution to the wars of national liberation has been its role as armorer. Due to the 'fraternal' support of the USSR and its allies, the MPLA in Angola and Frelimo in Mozambique managed to achieve and hold on to political power. Yet since independence, both countries have faced increasingly serious insurgencies from South African-backed rebels and the USSR now finds itself in the rather unusual role of seeking to preserve, rather than unseat, weak regimes. This transition from an insurgency to counterinsurgency power represents a dramatic reorientation for the Kremlin, in its Third World dealings. Soviet policymakers and Southern African elites have both come to realize that it is easier to destabilize than it is to defend and preserve. Indeed, socialist military assistance has had only limited success in protecting the frontline from South Africa.

In Angola, 30,000 Cuban troops along with possibly 1,000 Soviet officers have assisted the Angolan army in fighting against UNITA and the South African army. Although this support has not been enough to defeat Savimbi's forces, there is a degree of security for the capital and northern areas of the country. Most effective has been the establishment of a sophisticated network of radars and surface-to-air missile systems in Southern Africa which have successfully deterred attacks by the South African air force. A similar operation has been erected around Maputo in Mozambique.

However, Soviet assistance to Mozambique has been much less useful in preventing South African sponsored attacks. Renamo activity has spread throughout all of Mozambique's provinces, incurring serious damage and economic disruption. Although the Soviets have sent several teams of counterinsurgency experts to Mozambique, these efforts have not proven particularly successful. The USSR has threatened to take serious action over South Africa's role in the conflict, sending a convoy of ships to Maputo harbor in 1983, but this has not deterred Pretoria from engaging in efforts to wreak havoc upon Mozambique. Indeed, South Africa appears to have called the Soviet bluff in Mozambique while the USSR has concentrated its efforts to challenge the Republic in Angola. This is probably related, as much as anything, to the geographic proximity of Mozambique to South Africa and the relative distance separating Angola from the Republic.

While the USSR in particular has rendered valuable assistance to several of the frontline states in their struggles with South Africa, this support has not been without its problems. First, Soviet military hardware and personnel are often expensive, costing the Angolan government a good portion of the proceeds it earns each year from petroleum sales to the West. Second, the Soviet commitment to national survival for Marxist regimes in Southern Africa has been uneven, with the USSR adopting a generally lower profile in Mozambique since 1984. Third, the Soviet Union, while generous with its military support, has been unable to meet the economic needs of any of its allies in Southern Africa, and the West has generally withheld its economic and commercial assistance from these nations allied with the USSR. Fourth, and perhaps most serious, Soviet and South African military involvement in the region has created a cycle of reaction, whereby South African sponsored attacks spur an increase in Soviet military support which encourage further South African raids. True regional security in Southern Africa cannot be based solely on Soviet arms and Cuban troops.

Some Southern African countries, principally Zimbabwe, Zambia and Botswana, have foresworn security arrangements with the USSR in favor of close political and economic ties with the West. For instance, even though Zimbabwe had indulged in some anti-American votes in the United Nations, it receives more US foreign aid than any country in Southern Africa. This economic support for Zimbabwe has created a Western stake in its survival and success. On several occasions between 1981 and 1983, American diplomats registered strong complaints in Pretoria at South Africa's continuing campaign of economic sabotage against Zimbabwe. These attacks have in some cases been sharply curtailed. Most recently, after South African threats to invade Zimbabwe following a spate of ANC bombings, the US warned South Africa at the highest levels that such an attack would be viewed very unfavorably in Washington. Yet American influence on Pretoria has most certainly declined in recent months and the West's commitment to the frontline states is at best lukewarm. For example, Prime Minister Jonathan's pleas for Western

18

assistance to counter a military coup in Lesotho supported by South Africa fell on deaf ears.

A hallmark of South Africa's regional strategy in recent years has been the so-called nonaggression pact. In order to deny the ANC refuge in surrounding countries and to break out of diplomatic isolation on the African continent, the Republic has offered each of its neighboring states the option of forming a mutual pact to reject armed aggression. This invitation has often followed an unusually active period of South African-sponsored unrest in the chosen country. The most notable victory for this strategy was the Nkomati Accord, signed by Samora Machel and P.W. Botha in March 1984 (though South Africa had signed a similar agreement with Swaziland and a few years previously). Yet while Mozambique met the stipulations of Nkomati in regard to the ANC, South Africa's support for Renamo continued unabated. South African efforts to establish these 'peace' treaties have continued (South African officials have on several occasions extended the offer of a formal peace treaty to Angola), but Mozambique's experience raises serious questions about the Republic's willingness to adhere to any agreement which prohibits destabilization. It remains to be seen whether South Africa will now negotiate in good faith and respect the provisions of Nkomati. At this point, the ultimate utility of non-aggression pacts with South Africa have been called into question.

Probably the most surprising and successful effort to counter South African sponsored insurgency was the joint Zimbabwe-Mozambique military operation against Renamo. In a lightening strike on Renamo headquarters in August 1985, an estimated 6,000 Zimbabwean troops crossed the border and seized the rebel base known as Casa Banana. The rebel leader Alfonso Dhlakama managed to escape but his legions took serious casualties. The joint operation was well planned and executed and managed to surprise not only Renamo but South Africa as well. The development of a degree of military self-reliance in Zimbabwe has been clearly demonstrated and it suggests that indigenous regional security arrangements are likely to be an essential element in the achievement of real security in Southern Africa. (Yet clearly, the joint Zimbabwe-Mozambique military operation has not been without its problems, with Zimbabwe's military commanders openly disparaging of the effectiveness and discipline of Mozambique's troops.) Indeed bilateral, ad-hoc arrangements can be relatively simple to implement and many of the problems associated with large security groupings (expense, coordination and organization) can be gotten around. Local efforts at regional security have also tended not to be swept up by superpower rivalries. Informal military training arrangements between various frontline states have been stepped up in recent years and these exercises offer the possibility of greater coordination in any future joint maneuvers.

Despite the limited successes of many of these efforts to promote regional security in Southern Africa, the prospects of peace and security for the frontline states are not promising during this period of heightened turmoil in South Africa. The correlation of military and economic forces overwhelmingly favors Pretoria and will continue to do so for the foreseeable future. It is tempting to recommend that the frontline states follow a comprehensive strategy which comprises elements of each of the five measures discussed. Yet Mozambique, a country which has practiced each of these policies with varying degrees of commitment during its brief period of Independence is perhaps the least secure of any of the frontline states.

Zimbabwe's strategy of: maintaining close economic relations with the West; diversifying its military patrons to include Britain and North Korea; strengthening national military capabilities and bilateral defense cooperation with Mozambique; developing discreet lines of communication with Pretoria; and seeking not unfriendly relations with the USSR and its allies have all helped Zimbabwe to establish a degree of security. Given the current situation in South Africa, and the vast arsenal of power available to Pretoria, perhaps this is the best that can be expected or hoped for.

References

Arlinghaus, Bruce E. (ed.). *African Security Issues: Sovereignty, Stability and Solidarity*. (Colorado: Westview, 1984).

Clement, Peter. 'Moscow and Southern Africa', *Problems of Communism*. Vol. 34 (March/April 1985).

Crocker, Chester A. and Bissell, Richard E. (eds.). *South Africa into the 1980s.* (Colorado: Westview, 1979).

Hough, Jerry F. *The Struggle for the Third World.* (Washington: Brookings, 1986).

Jenkins, Simon; 'America and South Africa', *The Economist*, March 30, 1985.

————. 'Destabilization in Southern Africa', *The Economist*, July 16, 1983.

MacFarlane, Neil. 'Intervention and Regional Security'. *Adelph Paper*, No. 196, International Institute for Strategic Studies, London, 1985.

Price, Robert M. *US Foreign Policy in Sub-Saharan Africa: National Interest and Global Strategy.* (California: Institute of International Studies, 1978).

South Africa: Time Running Out. Report of the Study Commission on United States Policy Towards Southern Africa. (Berkeley: University of California, 1981).

PEACE AND ECONOMIC SECURITY CONSIDERATIONS IN SOUTHERN AFRICA

Ali Khalif Galaydh
Cambridge, Massachusetts

February 1986

Peace and economic security are scarce commodities in the Southern Africa of the 1980s. The Republic of South Africa (RSA) is still very much wedded to the dispossession, denationalization, dehumanization and other signature techniques of apartheid. Rather than implementing the stipulations of Security Council Resolution 435, South Africa defiantly occupies Namibia. Beyond the institutionalized racial repression inside its borders and the illegal and brutal occupation of Namibia, South Africa is pursuing a set of economic and military policies designed to ensure the imposition of its will on the majority-ruled states of the region. Peace is impossible in Southern Africa while apartheid obtains. The instruments of the Group Area Act, influx control, disenfranchisement and denationalization are being effectively challenged in the Republic as never before, at least in terms of the international mass media. The South African authorities, despite the declaration of an emergency, are unable to curb the urban violence, are impotent with regard to the school and consumer boycotts and are forced to reckon with the burgeoning black trade union movement. These recent manifestations of the anti-apartheid struggle have compounded the effects of the economic recession and undermined significantly the value of the Rand, and the credit-worthiness of the country. The long-term foreign investment climate has not been favorable for some time. The current inability to service its external debt coupled with the apparent political instability have led also to the drying up of new short-term foreign investment.

The economic and military dominance of South Africa in the region is incontrovertible. The monetary and fiscal policies of the Republic have direct bearing upon at least three states in the region. Its trade and investment policies are a salient feature of the economic statecraft of Southern Africa. Its railways, ports and tele-communications systems are a major component of the logistics and economic security of the whole subcontinent. And its mining industry and commercial agriculture are major employment sources for the labor markets of at least four neighboring states. The military might of the majority-ruled countries is no match, individually or collectively, for the South African Defense Forces. To illustrate the point, the budget of the South Africa defense establishment in 1984/85 was close to the Gross Domestic Product of Zimbabwe, which is second only to the Republic itself in terms of development. Asymmetrical trade and investment relations, significant employment opportunities, commanding logistics systems and dominant defense capabilities provide the Republic with a range of economic and military options in attempting to deflect external pressure emanating from its northern borders and to influence decisively the security and developmental decisions of its regional neighbors. The structural economic weaknesses, ravaging drought of recent years and incapacitating internal political divisions in some of the states have also enhanced the willingness and ability of South Africa to intervene. The regional response has been to establish the Southern Africa Development Coordination Conference (SADCC), which is a policy and programmatic attempt to reduce the dependency on South Africa and to promote coordinated development. The weakness of the Republic, on the other hand, lies manifestly as its core, and sanctions, like the sword of Damocles, hang uneasily over its head.

In examining the peace and economic security issues of the region an attempt will be made to focus on:

(A) economic hegemony exerted by South Africa over the region;

(B) the internal development problems in states in the region;

(C) the role of new regional institutions such as SADCC and PTA;

(D) the prospects for sanctions against the RSA, and

(E) the possible impact on these and other developments on the economies of the region.

(A) South African economic hegemony

The economy of the RSA has the distinct attributes of a dual economy. Aspects of it, such as industry, commercial agriculture, productivity and know-how, place it, in the terminology of the World Bank, in the ranks of the upper-middle income countries. Other aspects, such as subsistence agriculture, physical and social infrastructural facilities, particularly in the homelands, levels of skills and organization, production and incomes place it in the ranks of the least developed countries. This duality is a product, in the main, of apartheid. The relative deprivation of the non-white urban population and the absolute deprivation of some areas in the homelands are far from being lessened or even addressed adequately.[1] Be that as it may, the South African economy is dominant in size vis-á-vis the other countries of the region. This domination, which is reflected in the areas of infra-structure, trade and investment and employment varies among the states. It is greatest in Lesotho and Swaziland, and least in Tanzania and Angola. If the duality and other patterns of internal development are a product of political instruments, South Africa's economic relations with its neighbors are also very much determined, particularly in the last decade, by its political and security objectives. The use of economic relations first and foremost as political and security weapons underlies the quest for hegemony over the region.

The combined populations of the nine SADCC countries is twice that of the Republic, and their total land area is about four times as large. But their combined GDP is about a fourth and, more pertinently, their total foreign trade is only a third (Table I). The scope and intensity of industrialization differentiates it markedly from its neighbors. The industrial sector is the largest in

Table I. Southern African economies

	Population mid-1983	area ('000 square kms)	GNP per capita (US $) 1983	GNP average annual growth (%) 1965–1983	GDP (US $) 1983	Distribution of GDP (%) 1983			Merchandise Trade (Mil. US $) 1983		Terms of trade (1980 = 100)	
						Arg.	Manuf.	Service	Export 1983	Import 1983	1981	1983
Angola	8.2	1,247	470	– 2.3	2,500	48	3	29	1,859	768	110	99
Botswana	1.05	55	910	–	–	7.2	7.8	52.7				
Lesotho	1.5	30	460	6.3	300	23	6	55				
Malawi	6.6	118	210	2.2	1,330	43	13	37	220	312	106	126
Mozambique	13.1	802	230	– 0.1	2,360	44	9	40	260	635	96	96
Swaziland	0.6	17	680	–	–	25	24	44				
Tanzania	20.8	945	240	0.9	4,550	52	9	33	480	1,134	88	91
Zambia	6.3	753	580	– 1.3	3,350	14	19	48	866	690	81	82
Zimbabwe	7.9	391	740	1.5	4,730	11	21	57	1,273	1,432	–	–
South Africa	31.5	1,221	2,490	1.6	80,850	11	23	40	18,688	15,693	71	–

World Development Report, 1985.
World Development Report, 1983.
* GNP and GDP for Angola and Mozambique are for 1980.
* Merchandise trade of South Africa includes Namibia and BLS, but not between them.

terms of employment and contribution to GDP. Manufacturing alone is a close second to the service sector in terms of GDP contribution. Industrial consumer goods are an important component of the exports to the neighboring countries, and food, of which the Republic is a surplus producer, has proved to be of critical importance in regional relations. Broadly stated, the major economic linkages in the region are: (i) infrastructure, (ii) trade and investment and (iii) employment.

(i) *Infrastructure*[2]

The railways, roads, ports, air service, power grid and telecommunications of the RSA are very well developed and maintained. The mineral-producing hinterland is connected by rail and road to the older ports of Durban, Port Elizabeth, East London and Cape Town and to the newer, more specialized (coal and iron ore exports) ports of Richards Bay and Saldanha. There are also connections to the ports of Maputo, Mozambique, and Walvis Bay, Namibia. Inland, the system has extensions to the landlocked states of Botswana, Zimbabwe and Zambia. The cities and major towns of the country are connected by national and provincial highways which meet the passenger and freight requirements of the country. South African Airways services all the major centers, monopolizes the internal traffic and has, despite the denial of overflight rights by African states, an extensive foreign network. Prior to the construction of some new airports in some SADCC states, air travel among these states necessitated getting connecting flights from Johannesburg. The seven main ports of South Africa have the capacity to handle significantly more than the trading demands of the country. Their dry dock and repair facilities, bunkering, handling of specialized cargo, stevedoring, warehousing, and security make them very competitive. The reliable telex and telephone systems, shipping and forwarding capabilities, and developed rail and road networks for inland transport give the South African ports an added advantage. The ports, roads and airlines have been traditionally managed by the same state-owned organization that is responsible for the railways. The management of these national assets might be sound on efficiency and effectiveness standards, but 'railway diplomacy' also presents itself, all too clearly, as an option.

The ports of South Africa have never been the only ones in the region. The Mozambiquan ports of Maputo, Beira and Nacala are the most convenient ports for Swaziland, Malawi, Zimbabwe and Botswana. In fact, Maputo is the nearest port for the Transvaal, and has in part been developed with that in mind. On the Atlantic coast the Angolan port of Lobito has traditionally been the main port for the exports of Zaire and Zambia. These ports and their respective hinterlands are connected by a narrow-gauge railway system. The national liberation wars in Mozambique and Angola created serious problems for the rail transport system and thus reduced the volume of exports. The Unilateral Declaration of Independence by Rhodesia also had a serious effect on the Mozambiquan ports. Two new railway lines were installed: Tazara essentially for Zambian exports (copper) and imports, and a shorter line directly linking Zimbabwe to South Africa. The point is that it was only after the early 1970s, because of the anti-Portuguese national liberation wars and the imposition of sanctions against Rhodesia, that some rail traffic and exports were diverted to South Africa. The Angolan and Mozambiquan railways and ports suffered even more since independence at the hands of the Union for the Total Independence of Angola (UNITA) and the Mozambique National Resistance (MNR), the South African-supported dissident groups. The sabotage against the bridges, roads, railways and port facilities in Angola and Mozambique have necessitated the use of the South African infrastructure by the countries of the region, especially the land-locked. The increased reliance on the railways and ports of the Republic is a consequence of an interventionist policy of destabilization rather than an exercise of choice. The technical, managerial and financial problems of Dar es Salaam Port and Tazara do play a contributing role, but the push for a hegemonic relationship is grounded in the provision of an option and the concerted effort to eliminate the other viable options.

(ii) *Trade and investment*

Statistics on the trade and investment linkages between the RSA and the African countries are shrouded by political motivation and subterfuge. The strong linkages with SADCC, particularly Botswana, Lesotho and Swaziland (BLS), are more amenable to tracing. The BLS are part of the Southern African Customs Union (SACU), which dates back to 1910.[3] Lesotho and Swaziland are also members of the Rand Monetary Agency (RMA). Botswana used to be a member, and though the rand is not legal tender, it is a significant backer of the local currency. The monetary and fiscal policies of Lesotho and Swaziland, and to a lesser extent Botswana, are determined by the RSA. In 1981, roughly 5% of South Africa's exports were for the BLS and another 5.5% for other African countries, mainly SADCC.

Table II: Relative Importance of Regional Trade, 1981[4]

| | Exports (% of total) | | Imports (% of total) | |
	to SADCC	to RSA	from SADCC	from RSA
Angola	—	2	—	13
Botswana	9	17	6	88
Lesotho	—	—	—	95
Malawi	10	6	8	36
Mozambique	9	5	3	14
Swaziland	3	20	1	90
Tanzania	1	—	1	—
Zambia	4	1	5	16
Zimbabwe	10	17	6	22

The BLS are the most dependent on South African trade. Malawi, Mozambique, Zimbabwe, and increasingly Zambia are reliant on the Republic's exports. Industrial consumer goods, food and, more critically, energy are the major items. The BLS and Mozambique obtain electricity from the South African power grid. Malawi and Zimbabwe are forced to import oil products from South Africa when the Mozambiquan facilites are out of commission because of destabilization. The South African exports total roughly $2 billion annually while the imports are in the $300 million range. Zimbabwean manufactured exports (textiles, furniture and leather products) are about $100 million. The Republic gets 9% of its electricity from the Cabora Bassa complex and also uses the port of Maputo.

South Africa has extensive mining interests in Botswana and Zimbabwe. The internal trade of the BLS, and to a lesser extent of Zimbabwe, are also in the hands of South African firms. This has created, over the years, a product preference climate which is difficult to displace. The tourist industry of the SACU members, Malawi and Zimbabwe, are also dominated by the RSA. Two other factors also reinforce the trade and investment linkages. A significant number of the multinational corporations in most of SADCC operate out of the Republic. The shipping and forwarding agencies of South Africa (Manica and Rennies) have a very strong presence in six of the nine SADCC states, and are hardly expected to be indifferent to the maintenance of a dependency relationship. Obviously, the infrastructure and interventionist policies have an important influence also on the direction of trade.

(iii) *Employment*

Employment is another aspect of the asymmetrical relationship in the region. Labor from all the SADCC states has at one time or another sought work in the gold mines of South Africa (Table III). In recent history, however, the BLS, Mozambique, Malawi and Zimbabwe have provided labor for South Africa. In 1980, they accounted for 43.5% of the mine labor. The BLS have also provided labor on 'contractual arrangement' to commercial agriculture and other sectors. Lesotho alone accounted for 75,000 workers in commercial agriculture, in addition to the 96,300 in the mining industry.

Zimbabwe decided to discontinue the labor arrangement and South Africa has been trying to reduce its reliance on labor from SADCC. This policy decision has particularly affected Mozambique, which had almost 120,000 workers in 1975 and had under 40,000 in 1980. Lesotho has the highest stake in the exchange; some 200,000 of its citizens are gainfully employed in the Republic. Despite the effort to reduce the reliance on foreign migrant workers, South Africa has a vested interest in keeping them, at least those from the BLS. They are less prone to unionize and those who work in the gold mines are very skilled. Nonetheless, they are a 'lever' in the hands of those who manage the economic statecraft of the Republic. It was a 'disincentive'

Table III : Geographical sources of African mine labor, 1906–77[5]

	1906		1936		1970		1973		1977	
	('000)	%	('000)	%	('000)	%	('000)	%	('000)	%
South Africa	18.0	22.5	166.0	52	96.9	24.2	86	20.4	217.1	51.6
Lesotho	2.0	2.5	46.0	15	71.1	17.7	87	21.6	100	23.8
Botswana	0.3	0.4	7.0	2	16.3	4.1	17	4.0	24.8	5.9
Swaziland	0.6	0.7	7.0	2	5.4	1.3	5	1.2	11.8	2.8
Mozambique	53.0	66.4	88.0	28	113.3	28.2	99	23.5	38.2	9.1
Other	6.0	7.5	3.0	1	98.2	24.5	128	30.3	28.7	6.8
Total	79.9	100.0	318.0	100	401.2	100.0	422	100.0	420.5	100.0

used against Mozambique with devastating effect. None of the labor-exporting states have realistic reabsorption plans. In addition to the potential loss of remittances, unthinkable in the case of Lesotho, there is also the potential impact on internal peace and security.

(B) Internal development problems

Angola, Mozambique and Zimbabwe attained their independence, through armed struggle, in the last decade. FRELIMO won a clear military and political victory, but the economy was in tatters. The liberation war had left deep scars and the fleeing Portuguese settlers engaged in the massive destruction of infrastructure, factories and farm equipment.[6] Very few of the technical and professional staff stayed after independence. This posed enormous problems as there were hardly any nationals with the requisite skills after nearly four centuries of colonial rule. The Angolan economy has a large resource base but its level of development was no different. Whereas FRELIMO had no serious competitors, the MPLA was one of three liberation movements, each of which had its respective internal power bases and regional and inter-national supporters. The MPLA did win a military victory and would probably have achieved supremacy were it not for the continued external intervention. The internal conflict continues, and has given south Africa a convenient entry point. The internal conflict has become very much intertwined with the Namibian independence problem and has been transformed into a major international issue. The Angolan economy has not received much respite and does not command the full attention to the government as it is preoccupied with serious national security matters. Zimbabwe also has a history of armed struggle, but it is ultimately through the ballot box, after the Lancaster House negotiations, that ZANU won a stunning political victory. The sanctions imposed after the UDI had some beneficial effects on the development of the economy, primarily in the areas of food production and industry. The former High Commission Territories (BLS), Malawi, Zambia and Tanzania did not have similar traumatic experiences when they attained their independence in the 1960s.

Nor did they inherit an economy as developed or integrated as that of Zimbabwe.

The post-independence economic performance of the states in the region has not been impressive. The record of achievement is, however, positive in the development of physical and social intrastructure. Education, at the primary, secondary and even university levels, has been given the priority it deserves, after the decades (centuries in some cases) of colonial neglect. There are still some serious shortages in technical and professional areas, and these are targeted for the desired improvements. The investment outlays for health, though with distinct urban bias, and physical infrastructure (roads, railways, ports, electrical and water systems, telecommunications, etc.) have been very substantial, but the returns have been modest. The overall economic performances have been disappointing, particularly of late. The first (1960–1970) and second (1970–1980) United Nations Development Decades declared the goals of 5% and 6% of minimum annual rate of growth of aggregate national income for the developing countries. For the period 1965–1983, the GNP annual average growth rate was negative for Angola, Zambia and Mozambique (Table I). Lesotho had a 6.3% average growth rate and Malawi a 2.2%; others less. For the period 1980–1984, SADCC estimated that the per capita output of the member states fell by 15–20%.[7]

The reliance on one or a few commodities exposes the economies to the severe fluctuations of the world market. Four of the nine countries rely on one export item: Angola on oil, Botswana on diamonds, Zambia on copper and Lesotho on labor. Three rely on two or three products: Malawi on tobacco, tea and sugar; Mozambique on prawns and cashew nuts; and Swaziland on sugar and wood pulp. Tanzania and Zimbabwe have more diversified commodity exports. The terms of trade, particularly in the case of Zambia, have been mostly adverse. The oil price shocks, excluding Angola, and the high international interest rates have also had adverse effects. The external debts are relatively small by international standards, but debt servicing is nevertheless very burdensome. Weather has not been very cooperative either. The worst drought in a century had, in the past few years, a devastating effect on the whole region. It hastened the creeping environmental degradation and further enfeebled the fragile food production capacities. Zimbabwe, Malawi and even South Africa were forced to have large import bills of food; these have traditionally been the countries in the region with food surplusses (especially maize). Only Angola and Botswana have relatively comfortable foreign exchange positions; the drought and subsequent famine has exacerbated an already untenable balance of payments position in the other countries.

The inclement weather had a serious negative impact on the agriculture and agro-industries of the area, but the pronounced urban-biased development strategies had an equally serious impact on the agriculture and created the lop-sided development which characterizes most of the economies. Taken together, the pricing of agricultural inputs and outputs, the favoring of the small, politically powerful commercial agriculture in terms of allocations (credit, fertilizers, fuel, equipment and implements), the acquisition and distribution of 'food for peace' grants, and the over-valued currencies which enhance the proclivity for cheaper food imports have conspired against and worked havoc on food production, agricultural productivity and agricultural development in general. The internal terms of trade have been as adverse, if not worse, as the external ones. Industrialization via import-substitution had some initial successes. The expected internal linkages did not, however, prove to be strong. On the contrary, the need for inputs (spares, expertise, etc.) has increased the external dependency and, in the face of chronic foreign exchange shortages, most plants have been condemned to operate below capacity. Internal competition has been barred by structural obstacles, and high tariffs have precluded external competition. These capital-intensive and high-cost infant industries have not led to industrial growth and development or, for that matter, to self-reliance. High production costs and over-valued currencies militate against export potential and the internal markets are, in most countries, very small. Industrialization had the pride of place in the development strategies pursued, and its stunted growth has had debilitating effects on other sectors. Mismanagement and corruption have taken their toll on the early post-independence optimism and, apart from their effects on economic performance, have also contributed to the apparent contraction of the human spirit.

The economies of the SADCC states are not in an enviable position. Low rates of growth and development, which cannot even keep up with the population increases in some of the countries, stagnating food production, decreasing foreign aid, mounting debt servicing problems and inclement weather have put them, in recent years, in a bind. It is difficult as it is, in both economic and security terms. More than 100,000 people died of starvation in Mozambique during the recent drought. There is hardly any security when the most basic of needs, human life, cannot be saved — and in such numbers. South Africa's intervention, active economic manipulation, support of dissident groups and cross-border armed agression, had a devastating impact on the peace and economic security of the region. The cost of South African destruction and destabilization during the past five years has been put at $10 billion.[8] That is more than the combined foreign aid to SADCC during the same period, and would most probably be more than the total for the next decade. What is not given a price, however, is the increasing delegitimization activities. The crossing of borders by the SADF with impunity, commando destruction of major facilities, and the imposition of crippling economic embargoes do not endear the target states to their populations. Another example of attempted delegitimization is that of Radio Truth, aimed at Zimbabwe; this is a new weapon that has not been used with much effect before. The most graphic example of South African intervention is the forcing out of the civilian government of Lesotho last month. Lesotho has been known to be the most vulnerable of the SADCC countries, but the naked exercise of South African power is a testimony to the aggressive stance of that country in regional relations. Peaceful negotiations and the voluntary entrance into non-aggression pacts (UN Resolution 435, Lusaka Accords and Nkomati) are apparently not sufficient. South Africa in its purported counter-insurgency campaigns occupies parts of Angola, and the death and destruction, at the hands of the South African-created and supported MNR, are unabated in Mozambique. Namibia is still illegally occupied.

(C) The role of the new regional institutions

The majority-ruled states of Southern Africa belong to two main regional organizations: (a) the Southern Africa Development Coordination Conference (SADCC) and (b) the Preferential Trade Area. SADCC grew out of the coordination of the diplomatic and political activities of the frontline states (Angola, Botswana, Mozambique, Zambia and Tanzania). While the objective reasons for regional economic coordination and integration were present, the subjective impetus perhaps was provided by the serious interest shown by the South African government in forming a Constellation of Southern African States (CONSAS). This was to be made up of the countries south of the Zambezi and the Kunene rivers, including the homelands. The frontline states perceived this to be an attempt to thwart their quest for economic liberation, hijack the liberation of Zimbabwe and Namibia, and engineer diplomatic recognition for the homelands. The SADCC formation preempted this ambitious design of the RSA. SADCC, in a sense, was then a 'counter constellation', but the rationale for its formation goes much beyond this defensive move. The development objectives of the organization are: [9]

   a) the reduction of economic dependence, particularly, but not only, on the Republic of South Africa;
   b) the forging of links to create a genuine and equitable regional integration;
   c) the mobilization of resources to promote the implementation of national, interstate and regional policies; and
   d) concerted action to secure international cooperation within the framework of our strategy for economic liberation.

Reducing the dependency relationship with South Africa and promoting regional economic integration are the irreducible goals of SADCC. Reducing the dependency on the Republic is not confined to the creation of an alternative to the present unequal exchange, but also entails checking the centripetal economic forces at work. The political consequences of the established economic dependency have posed, invariably, a clear and ever-present danger to the peace and security of the area. The promotion of regional integration does not translate into a common market, nor does it mean the installation of an elaborate bureaucratic mechanism. Rather, the approach is that of muddling through.

A tiny secretariat, with annual membership contributions of $50,000, is neither capable of formulating regional integration plans and programs, nor mandated to do so. Apart from the general goals of reducing dependency and increasing regional cooperation and integration, the organization has a program of action in the areas of transport and communication, animal health, food security, agricultural research, industry, energy, training and the establishment of a development fund. Each member state was made responsible for one subject or sub-subject area. The technical coordination units established in member states, and the secretariat, have no decision-making powers. Each state is ultimately responsible for the selection, funding and execution of the projects in its domain, while taking SADCC's priorities into consideration. Regional decisions are made by censensus among the states and, once made, are upheld. The muddling through approach is time-consuming and has other built-in deficiencies. On the other hand, the approach has facilitated the carving out of the obvious areas of cooperation and the avoidance of serious conflict areas.

For a regional organization which is only five years old, SADCC should be considered a success. It has identified some 400 projects costing about $5 billion. Despite the very serious drop in foreign aid in the past decade, SADCC has been able to secure over $1 billion in foreign aid; another $1.25 billion are under negotiation. Not all of these projects or funds are attributable to SADCC. Some pre-date SADCC, but other major funds would not have been granted without SADCC. The transport projects are a case in point. Of the total funds that have been secured, OECD has provided about 73%. The Scandinavian and Benelux countries have provided the largest share of the funds secured. i.e. 52.2%.[10] The major OECD countries, the US, the UK, Germany, France, Japan and Canada, have not been active supporters. Nor are the World Bank, the EEC, and the UNDP.

The Preferential Trade Area, with a potential of twenty East and Southern African states, has been evolving for a much longer time than SADCC. It is sponsored by the United Nations Economic Commission for Africa (ECA); its main objectives are to reduce and/or eliminate tariff and non-tariff barriers among the member states. Its long-term aims are to establish a common market and an economic community. The PTA is thus different from SADCC in its objectives and in its approach. It is not as decentralized as SADCC; it is headquartered in Lusaka and has a clearing facility in Harare. Whereas SADCC promotes production in order to push trade, the PTA promotes trade in order to pull production; and whereas the former is in favor of counter-trade, the latter favors free trading and having a clearing house facility in the transitional period. These apparent differences in objectives and approaches pose some problems for SADCC members who are also members, or are eligible to become members, of the PTA. Zambia and Zimbabwe are very strong supporters of the PTA while Tanzania, Angola, Mozambique and Botswana have only recently ratified the PTA instruments. SADCC itself does not have an official view on the matter.

(D) The prospects of sanctions against the RSA

Sanctions are coercive measures taken against a state which violates international law. South Africa's apartheid system, which is institutionalized racial oppression, is in clear violation of the United Nations Charter. The human rights and fundamental freedoms of over 85% of the total population are brutally and systematically denied. All aspects of this international opprobrium are enshrined in pervasive laws. The question is not whether sanctions should be imposed, because the destabilization and cross-border incursions of the SADF are obviously acts of aggression that violate regional peace, and because the occupation of Namibia is a blatant breach of international peace, but what type of sanctions should be applied. Since Longbenton Urban Council, a British local authority, imposed sanctions against South Africa in May 1958 and since Jamaica became the first state to impose such sanctions in July 1959, governmental and non-governmental organizations, in increasingly large numbers, have resorted to such punitive measures. The United Nations, since the early 1960s, has been grappling with what type of sanctions would be appropriate. The General Assembly passed a resolution in November 1962 urging member states to break off diplomatic relations and to end trading and transport linkages with South

Africa. The Security Council adopted a resolution in 1963 stipulating a voluntary arms embargo. Another Security Council resolution calling for mandatory arms embargo was passed in 1977.[11]

The type and scope of sanctions is a function of the internal developments in the Republic. The Sharpville massacre in 1961 prompted the spate of sanctions in the early 1960s. Soweto and the murder of Steve Biko had a similar, though more pronounced, impact in the 1970s. The organized opposition to apartheid and the subsequent inability of the regime to control the violence in the last eighteen months, have galvanized support for taking more far-reaching punitive measures. That support is most critical in the countries which have major investment, trade and security stakes. These are the countries of North America and Western Europe, headed by the US, the UK and the Federal Republic of Germany. The sustained non-violent struggle against the overwhelming instruments of racial repression has influenced significantly the public opinions of these countries. In the US, the moral outrage against the carnage palpably portrayed by television has caught the imagination of college students, church groups and citizens' committees. Their enormous energies have been channelled to put pressure on Congress and on the firms that have investments in South Africa. Some universities, city and state governments, and trade unions have responded to the campaign for divestment and the pressure to disinvest. Even the Reagan Administration has felt the political heat, and with its 'constructive engagement' in ruins, primarily because of South African intransigence, it was forced to adopt a milder form of sanctions than the one passed by Congress.

The Reagan, Thatcher and Kohl administrations are not known for their unswerving commitment against South Africa, yet the American government, the Commonwealth and the European Community have established a set of punitive measures against the Republic. It is, granted, a minimalist set of measures, but what Samuel Johnson said about dogs who walk on their hind legs comes to mind: 'The wonder is not that they do it badly but they do it at all'! Time seems not to be on South Africa's side; the momentum has definitely turned against it in the past year. Constructive engagement appears to have been the final attempt at diplomatic prodding; armed confrontation supported by the international community is not in the cards. Cultural, sporting, political and economic sanctions, in the absence of other viable non-violent options, are the only means available to push South Africa to dismantle apartheid. The scope and intensity of the punitive measures have been changing recently and still have some distance to go in order to be effective.

(E) The possible impact of sanctions

The non-violent struggle of the last two years has exposed the internal weakness of South Africa. The consumer and school boycotts, the strikes by the African trade unions, the formation of decentalized and democratic organizations, and the apparent ungovernability of the townships have been instrumental in the orchestration of consciousness. The consumer boycott, particularly during the past Christmas season, has compounded the recession problems. The boycott and the dismaying general state of affairs have alarmed the business community. Prominent segments of the business community are emphatically trying to distance themselves from the government, and some are even pressing for a separate peace with the anti-apartheid forces. Apparently, the present disincentives are having some of the desired impact, at least amongst the business community. The informal embargo by international bankers, mostly Americans, has further aggravated the perceived weakness. The inability to service the external debts has pulled the rug from under the rand and led to its collapse.

These latest developments confirm that South Africa is not immune to the impact of sanctions. Sanctions by themselves will not lead to the demise of apartheid. But no other viable options which could realistically bring about the dismantling of apartheid are available. That comparative perspective has to be borne in mind when assessing the impact of negative sanctions. The effectiveness of sanctions will depend on (a) the timing, (b) the scope and (c) internal developments. The timing of imposing sanctions against the RSA is crucial because catching it in an economic recession would increase the costs. Such timing would prolong the down-turn — which would depress production and domestic investment and would increase the ranks of the unemployed. The scope of sanctions pertains not only to how comprehensive they are, but also to how much support there is for them. A comprehensive embargo which covers trade, investment and military cooperation is bound to have more impact than selective sanctioning. A mandatory embargo adhered to by the major partners (the US, UK, Germany and Japan) would have a better chance of incurring unacceptable costs than a voluntary embargo. Internal economic and political developments would also affect and be affected by the impact of sanctions. Well-timed, comprehensive and mandatory sanctions, coupled with organized internal struggles, would impose unacceptable costs on the apartheid system. How long the system would withstand the costs of non-compliance is not easy to predict. On the other hand, without sanctions the continued survival of apartheid would not be seriously challenged. The impact of sanctions on (a) South Africa, (b) neighboring states, and (c) Western countries will be examined very briefly.

(i) *South Africa*

The country has been bracing itself for the eventuality of sanctions. The attaining of self-sufficiency has been a major objective, especially in the areas of energy, food and some basic industries. The growth of the country in the past three decades has been export-led. Some 75% of its export proceeds are from minerals, and gold alone accounts for some 50%. The kruggerrand sales accounted for about 12% of gold production in 1984, but that market has collapsed because of the ban. Sanctions against gold would not be easy but other minerals, particularly coal and iron-ore, are very vulnerable. France and Italy have been the major importers of South African coal and France has recently decided not to renew its contract. Foreign investment still has a significant role to play in the growth of the economy, and its denial would have a serious braking effect. The economy relies heavily on a wide range of imported technology, not only computers. Some of the industries which were billed to increase self-sufficiency (e.g., SASOL) are very much reliant on foreign suppliers. Oil imports account for 15—20% of the total energy consumption. The country obtains oil from the spot market but with a mandatory embargo this would be a more costly transaction. An embargo on the foreign trade and investment of the country, even if it is not 100% effective, would, at a minimum, wipe out growth in the economy. Unemployment would be a serious problem. Since the impact on the people would be serious, the authorities would try to ensure differential impact. The African people seem to be prepared for that outcome and are in agreement with the statement of the late Albert Luthule', . . . if a temporary hardship is a way of removing a permanent suffering, it is the price we are gladly prepared to pay'.[12]

(ii) *Neighboring states*

A mandatory embargo on South Africa would have a direct impact on the BLS. As members of both SACU and the RMA, Lesotho and Swaziland would experience enormous monetary and fiscal problems. Botswana is also a member of SACU and would face similar fiscal problems. The case of Lesotho would be extreme because it is dependent completely on the ports and the transport system of the Republic. The BLS and four other SADCC members are dependent, to varying degrees, on South African trade and investment. A down-turn in the Republic's economy would affect its trading partners and would lead also to the loss of jobs in the gold mines. Lesotho again would be an extreme case: 200,000 of its citizens are workers in South Africa. Another possible impact is that of 'a mad dog scenario'. South Africa would be expected to use its 'railway diplomacy' and other economic countermeasures in order to maintain its hegemony. The Republic, in desperation, might try to use all-out violence to force SADCC members to help in circumventing the embargo. There is even talk, *sotto voce*, of nuclear blackmail.

(iii) *Western countries*

The OECD countries are the major trading partners of South Africa. The US, the UK and the Federal Republic of Germany also have substantial investments in the country. The loss of exports would lead to some unemployment, but the cost would hardly be unbearable. The volume of new investment has been

So What did SADCC achieve in its
transport sector? A

41

relatively small in recent years, and therefore there would be very little opportunity cost. Loss of income from previous investments would be large, but would depend on the countermeasures taken by South Africa. The Republic provides roughly 60% of the world gold exports. The price of gold has fluctuated widely in recent years and mandatory sanctions would increase the volatility. This in turn would have a major impact on the international monetary system. Newly mined gold, however, is very small in quantity compared to the existing monetary gold and private gold stocks. An increased measure of demonetizing gold prior to the embargo would be a boost to its effectiveness. The OECD countries also rely on some South African minerals (manganese, platinum, chrome, vanadium, etc.) for which there are no other main sources or readily available substitutes. The quantities required are, however, small, and prudent stockpiling would blunt a strategic mineral denial posture by South Africa.

Conclusion

The peace and economic security of the majority-ruled Southern African states are under enormous strain. Their economies are in a bind because of unequal exchange in the international market, ravaging drought and destabilization carried out by their southern neighbor. The urban-biased development strategy pursued by these countries is in part to blame, particularly in food production. South Africa's politically motivated economic manipulation, illegal occupation of Namibia, and cross-border armed aggressions are a clear and ever-present danger to the regional peace. Internal conflicts, obviously, provide the SADF with convenient entry points, as in the case of UNITA. Even where there is no serious internal conflict, the Republic 'rents' a movement. The MNR is, for all practical purposes, a rented movement.

The majority-ruled countries have opted to form SADCC in order to enhance their bargaining position, reduce their dependency on the RSA and promote integrated regional development. The decentralized structure and muddling through approach of SADCC are in sharp contrast to the structure and objectives of the PTA, which is another regional organization for the Eastern the two organizations pose some serious problems for regional integrated development. In South Africa itself peace and security are also under attack. The recent internal challenges to apartheid have exposed the inherent weaknesses of the system. That has encouraged the anti-apartheid forces, inside and out, but it has alarmed the South African and international business communities. Even the international bankers realize the need for fundamental political changes. The call for further sanctions is gaining momentum. Mandatory sanctions would play a contributing role to the total strategy of dismantling apartheid. Sanctions would have costs for South Africa, neighboring states and major trading partners of the Republic. The African people in the RSA and its neighboring states are willing to absorb these costs, because there are no other options with lesser costs.

Notes

1. An adequate portrayal of the deprivation of homelands is provided in Hermann Giliomee and Lawrence Schlenner, eds., *Up Against the Fences: Poverty, Passes and Privilege in South Africa* (New York: St. Martin's Press, 1985).
2. The following discussion is based upon Robert I. Rotberg, *Suffer the Future* (Cambridge, Massachusetts: Harvard University Press, 1980), pp. 17–23; and Joseph Hanlon, 'SADCC: Progress, Projects and Prospects', the Economist Intelligence Unit: Special Report #182 (1984).
3. On SACU and the RMA, see Gavin Maasdorp, 'New Groupings in Southern Africa: PTA and SADCC', in Alternative Structures for Southern African Interaction (Africa Institute of Southern Africa).
4. Hanlon, p. 70.
5. Francis Wilson, 'Mineral Wealth and Rural Poverty', in Giliomee and Schlenner, p. 58 and Anon J. Nsekela, ed., *Southern Africa: Toward Economic Liberation* (London: Rex Collings, 1981), p. 211.
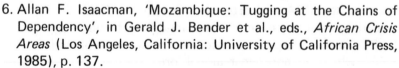
6. Allan F. Isaacman, 'Mozambique: Tugging at the Chains of Dependency', in Gerald J. Bender et al., eds., *African Crisis Areas* (Los Angeles, California: University of California Press, 1985), p. 137.

7. 'SADCC: Back-Slapping', in *African Confidential*, vol. 27, no. 1 (January 2, 1986), p. 6.
8. *Ibid.*, p. 6.
9. Nsekela, p. 3.
10. Elaine A. Friedland, 'The Southern African Development Coordination Conference and the West', in the Journal of Modern African Studies, vol. 27, no. 2 (June 1985), p. 289.
11. Tony Koenderman, *Sanction: The Threat to South Africa* (Johannesburg: Jonathan Bell Publishers, 1982), p. 27.
12. Cited in Koenderman, p. 50.

SOME THOUGHTS ON PRECONDITIONS NECESSARY FOR A MEDIATED SETTLEMENT BY THE UNITED NATIONS IN NAMIBIA

Victor Umbricht
The Mediator, East African Community

(A) Introduction

The writer of the following 'thoughts' was invited, in view of his African experience, to provide some ideas which might help in reaching a mediated settlement in Namibia. The mode for such a settlement is described as *'mediated* by the *UN.'* Why a mediation? and why by the UN? I shall examine these and other questions which might be explored as avenues to lead to independence in Namibia. The only objective which ultimately matters is to find a generally and voluntarily accepted understanding on Namibian independence, based on equity, fairness and respect for human rights. It must take into account historical developments and sober research of facts, and avoid, if possible, the pitfalls of political opportunity or of power grabbing.

(B) History and background

General historical background

As a geographical area, Namibia (then South West Africa) came into being during the last two decades of the 19th century as a result of agreements between Britain, Portugal and Germany. This border settlement was the culmination of Germany's desire in 1884 to acquire a colony in southwestern Africa. This area, known as German Southwest Africa, did not include the Walvis Bay and the coastal strip, as this had been annexed by Britain in 1878 and was part of the Cape Colony. The latter became the property of South Africa.

In 1915, at the onset of World War I, troops from South Africa invaded German Southwest Africa and placed it under military administration until 1921, when it became a Class C mandated territory administered by South Africa on behalf of the League of Nations. The Class C Mandate authorized administering governments (i.e., South Africa) to excise full powers over the territories concerned as an integral part of their own state. This, of course, was subject to the authority of the Council of the League of Nations.

In 1946, the delegation of the Union of South Africa submitted a proposal to the General Assembly of the UN calling for approval of the *annexation* of South West Africa by the Union of South Africa. The General Assembly rejected South Africa's proposal and instead recommended that the territory be placed under international trusteeship. South Africa refused.

Serious criticism continued to be raised in the UN by the countries of the Third World against the unilateral way South Africa was carrying out its mandate. South Africa denied this and Liberia and Ethiopia brought the case before the International Court of Justice for legal interpretation of the clauses in the mandate, which was rendered in 1966.

In 1966, the UN General Assembly adopted Resolution 2145, declaring that the mandate was terminated until such time as it attained independence. The next year, the Assembly created an 11-member Council for South West Africa and soon thereafter renamed the territory Namibia.

The UN severely reprimanded South Africa again in 1971 for having profoundly violated the spirit of the mandate by having introduced apartheid in Namibia. These apartheid laws were abrogated again in 1977, although not completely, some governmental institutions (schools, hospitals) remaining reserved for white people only.

Comparison with other African independence movements

The South African policy of incorporation changed in the 1970s under the pressure of labor unrest and guerrilla clashes in Namibia and of outside events. First among the latter was the Portuguese withdrawal from Angola and the establishment of the MPLA government which provided a base outside Namibia for SWAPO's operations, while South Africa allied herself with UNITA in opposition to the MPLA and carried out a fruitless invasion of the country. At the same time, on the domestic front, South Africa was faced with a series of riots and other forms of protest from its own black population. Internationally, there was soon a visible change in American policy with the arrival in 1977 of the liberal Carter administration. South Africa could no longer rely on even tacit US approval and powerful American support.

In the face of the combined pressure of these developments on all fronts, South Africa abandoned its policy of incorporating Namibia into the Republic and set about seeking an internal settlement based on ethnic authorities (a variation of the homelands policy) in the hope that it would create an independent state on its borders which would not cause difficulties for South Africa.

While the constitutional steps taken by the South African government following the Turnhalle Conference were certainly not adequate for bringing meaningful independence and could not have been accepted as a lasting solution, this change of direction in South African policy was important and could have been a significant turning point. With the benefit of hindsight, it is possible to see this as an opportunity missed. It offered a chance to develop a reform movement from within, taking what was on offer and keeping up the pressure for more constitutional advances until full independence was secured, primarily by peaceful means (the strategy adopted by many other African independence movements). But the elections at the end of 1978 were boycotted by SWAPO and some other small parties. As a consequence, South Africa could always make the point thereafter that SWAPO, by its uncompromising rejection (understandable as that might be), lost the opportunity of influencing events from within.

Instead, SWAPO relied on international support, especially in the UN. A resolution rejecting the philisophy of ethnic authorities and calling for non-ethnic elections under UN supervision was adopted unanimously by the Security Council in January 1976 (shortly after the Turnhalle Conference) as SCR 385. This was a notable declaration of principle, but did not in itself change the position in Namibia. It needed to be translated into action. At this juncture, the five western powers who were then members of the Security Council (The Contact Group) took the initiative to draw up an implementation plan after consultation with 'the various parties involved with the Namibian situation.'

It envisaged elections to a Constituent Assembly, the drawing up and adoption of an independence constitution and the appointment of a UN Special Representative, assisted by a UN Transition Assistance Group (UNTAG) with civilian and military components, to supervise and ensure free and fair elections. It spelled out certain 'prior requirements,' such as the repeal of the remaining discriminatory laws, the release of political prisoners and detainees, the peaceful return of refugees, and the 'cessation of all hostile acts,' including the return of all forces to base and phased withdrawal of most South African forces from Namibia within 12 weeks. This settlement plan was adopted as Resolution 435 in September 1978.

In the course of the following months, these principles were accepted by all parties including South Africa, SWAPO and the frontline states. Despite this widespread acceptance, despite much discussion, clarification and amplification of particular points and certain significant agreements (notably the 'Principles concerning the Constituent Assembly and the Constitution for an independent Namibia,' put forward by the Contact Group in July 1982), no cease-fire was agreed and elections for a Constituent Assembly seem as far off as ever. The efforts of the Contact Group have run into the ground and there is stalemate. Why is this?

Special factors in Namibia

Before attempting to answer this question it would be useful to recall some of the factors which have made, and continue to make, the progress of the territory towards independence different from that of almost all other African countries and more difficult. Some of the many factors in the background of the current situation are the following:

(a) The fact that the administering power did not have independence as a goal for the short or long term until the 1970s. For decades, South Africa was effectively pursuing a policy of annexation. Far from preparing Namibia for independence, the reverse was the aim.
(b) Namibia's status as a mandated territory gave the UN a direct role from the start.
(c) The refusal of the mandatory to recognise UN jurisdiction added a further and major complication.
(d) The application of apartheid and 'homelands' policies, even if not to the same degree as in South Africa itself. Few other dependent territories experienced racial discrimination in such an extreme form.
(e) The presence of a long-established and economically powerful settler community, increased more recently by a less stable and less pragmatic South African commercial mining and administrative community. This both delayed the appearance of an articulate and organized nationalist movement and made it the fiercer when it arrived.
(f) Maldistribution of land between immigrant settlers and native cultivators, in conjunction with a contract labor system under state control.
(g) Imprisonment of nationalists for very long terms, which weakened leadership to no party's advantage.
(h) Prolonged armed struggle.
(i) As the last non-independent country in Africa, Namibia draws upon the support of the rest of the continent. Namibian independence, therefore, did not remain an issue between Namibia and South Africa, or even a Southern Africa issue for the neighbouring frontline states, but early turned into a regional issue of Africa-wide concern on the OAU agenda.
(j) The relationship of the nationalists with neighboring Angola

and the central role of the UN has brought an East-West dimension to the problem.

Many of these features applied to numerous other African countries, but the *combination* of all in Namibia must be unique. What does all this imply for the prospects of settlement? In the first place, it means that the positions of the parties are more than usually sharply opposed, long-standing and deep-rooted. Secondly, because the dispute has been so protracted, positions taken up at any stage can easily become out-dated, but if taken up publicly, it is difficult for any party to surrender or even modify them quickly to meet changing circumstances. Thirdly, there is an unusually large number of 'interested parties.' It may well be the case that not all of them can be accommodated in an independence settlement, but a settlement would have to be such that it did not rule out the possibility of accommodation for all, in parallel negotiations, if necessary.

The position of the UN

The position of the UN at the centre of the Namibian question deserves further consideration. Does this help, or hinder a settlement? What are the implications?

(a) It has meant that there was early recourse to legal processes and the International Court of Justice, which established:
  — the continuation, post World War II, of the mandate, UN to replace LN, all other provisions unchanged;
  — the admissibility of petitions to the UN;
  — the validity of the termination of the mandate in 1966 by the General Assembly (1971 opinion).
Nevertheless, South Africa continues to maintain that its presence in Namibia is not illegal. Thus, pronouncements from the highest legal authority have had little apparent influence in practice.

(b) It has meant that there were early pressures for sanctions, reinforcing the call for sanctions on account of South Africa's domestic policies:

— arms embargo, observed more or less, but without decisive results; South Africa has an efficient armaments industry, so is not deprived of weaponry, it only becomes more expensive;

— repeated and continuing calls for mandatory economic sanctions, especially an oil embargo; there are well-known differences of view as to the possibility of applying sanctions effectively and historical experience casts doubt on their efficacy; at some point, continued pressure for economic sanctions will become counter-productive, if it has not reached that point already.

(c) Assumption by the UN of administrative and legislative responsibility through the UN Council for Namibia; this was a logical sequence of the termination of the mandate and was necessary to fill the vacuum it left, but:

— again it illustrates the disparity between the UN's powers *de jure* and *de facto*, which weakens UN standing;

— it also means that the UN is no longer an impartial third party which can hold the ring, but a principal in the question.

(d) The early recognition by the UN (1967) of SWAPO as 'sole and authentic representative of the Namibian people' may have been and may continue to be detrimental to progress. At minimum it gives South Africa a plausible argument to question UN impartiality. More seriously, insistence on maintaining its 'sole' position is a divisive factor in the independence struggle. This could have harmful long-term effects; experience shown that divisions between exiles and those who stayed behind are obstacles in nation-building. There is room for conscientious differences of view on the use of the bullet (whether along with or in place of the ballot), and room for attempts at national reconciliation and the creation of a united front of the internal and external parties (not necessarily an agreement on all points, but united to achieve independence).

(e) Deliberation of the issues in the General Assembly and more particularly in the Security Council means that the danger is ever present that the Namibian question is treated as simply an element in East-West rivalry. The so-called Cuban question is only one obvious example of the clouding of the fundamental issue.

(C) Failure to implement Resolution 435

Until this day, Resolution 435 has not been implemented, despite being accepted in 1978 by all parties, including South Africa and SWAPO. What are the reasons behind this failure?

1. Three main objects have been raised by South Africa:
   (a) The first and most serious obstacle was the introduction of the so-called 'Cuban link.' South Africa, supported by the US for its own reasons, demands that the Cuban troops in Angola be withdrawn prior to Namibian elections. South Africa claims that the presence of large Cuban forces and 'advisers' from the Eastern bloc in neighboring Angola could be used in support of SWAPO forces to influence and even intimidate the Namibian electorate and sway a vote towards SWAPO. This would be a violation of the principle of free elections and free expression of political affiliation (not to mention facilitating SWAPO's accession to power — an event which South Africa would do much to prevent).

   (b) South Africa has little confidence in the *impartiality of the UN* in general, and in the Security Council in particular. It fears that the UN troops, who are instructed to oversee the fairness of the elections, might be inclined to side with SWAPO — 'the sole and authentic representative of the Namibian people' — and thus also assist, however, invisibly, in swinging elections in SWAPO's direction.

   (c) Another hindrance results from the issue of when (in South Africa's view, *after* the departure of the Cubans) Resolution 435 should be carried out. South Africa is *opposed* to *immediate* implementation, and does not accept deadlines for independence. It has formulated the proposition that SWAPO should first end all guerrilla activity in Northern Namibia and operate in Namibia as a political party — just like the other internal parties. Thereafter, the internal parties and SWAPO should sit down together and determine jointly the further process in a Roundtable Conference.

These Roundtable discussions would have to be unconditional, i.e., all parties together would decide whether they still favor the implementation of Resolution 435 as it stands, or whether a different course of action towards full independence would be more appropriate. This procedure would of course be time-consuming. In this approach, South Africa does not reject SCR 435, but claims to be seeking a better way towards independence, if such could be agreed between South Africa, SWAPO, the internal parties and the frontline states.

2. Not surprisingly, SWAPO has rejected all these suggestions and maintained its position as before:
   (a) Linkage, which does not figure in Resolution 435, is held to be an extraneous element; the presence of Cuban forces in Angola is regarded as a matter between these two governments only.

   Although the Cuban link is of course rejected by SWAPO, (as it is by the FLS and most of the Contact Group) as a pre-condition for implementation, all of them and practically all other African countries would welcome the departure of every foreign military contingent from every country. Moreover, it is acknowledged that a connection exists in practice. For its part, Angola has given the impression in public statements in 1984–85 that it accepts a gradual Cuban withdrawal conditionally, the conditions being that South Africa does the same in Angola *and* in Namibia. Angola's view is that such a withdrawal would also imply an end to all guerrilla activity by UNITA, against whom Cuban military help is required. If this impression has been correctly relayed, it constitutes a significant development that could usefully serve as a point of departure for a Namibian settlement.

   (b) In the SWAPO view, Resolution 435 has to be implemented without dilution, i.e., withdrawal of South African troops from Namibia, and replacement by UN troops, UN-supervised elections and a new constitution.

(c) Resolution 435 has to be implemented immediately; SWAPO does not propose to share its role as 'sole and authentic representative of the Namibian people' with other, internal parties; and its guerrilla activities have to continue until final victory.

In the meantime, South Africa has pressed ahead with the inauguration of a new interim internal administration in Windhoek in conjunction with members of the internal parties, retaining the position of Administrator-General but transferring certain powers other than defense and foreign affairs to an 'interim central government.' South Africa claims these are transitional arrangements until internationally recognized independence is achieved, but the moves have been interpreted as a unilateral attempt to set up a client regime in Namibia and condemned almost universally, by SWAPO, the FLS and the Contact Group. This is a further obstacle to implementation of Resolution 435.

(D) Fact-finding as pre-condition for a settlement

If experience is any guide, it teaches us that any settlement of such historic dimensions as accession to full independence will be on safer ground and bring more lasting benefit to the people if 'the facts of life' are carefully weighed, mainly aspects such as: economic facts; social facts; institutional facts; and facts for consideration in a new constitution.

A comprehensive fact-finding effort characterized by total integrity, objectivity and impartiality is, in the eyes of this writer, an indispensable pre-condition for meeting the justified expectation of the entire population of state achieving independence; the absence of solid factual knowledge will jeopardize any endeavors to strike a well-pondered balance between the various groups in a state and could well give rise to such adverse consequences as tribal frictions, political and economic unrest, disregard for minorities, etc.

Needless to say, much data has been gathered by the United Nations, the Commonwealth Secretariat, the Secretariats of the Organization of African Unity and the Economic Commission for Africa, by the Commonwealth Group of Eminent Persons and by other bodies. Any experienced mediator will, of course, turn to all those sources in possession of relevant factual information.

Nonetheless, there are disputed facts, reflecting both the lack of direct access to the territory, as well as the reliability, in the eyes of certain parties, of information gathered by an organization which supports one of the main actors in the dispute. An illustration of the need for fact-finding concerns, for example, an exchange of views reported by the media to have taken place in 1984 on the island of Cape Verde between South Africa, the US and Angola to renew efforts for a solution of the thorny question of the 'Cuban Departure.' The outcome has not been made public, but reliable sources have come to the conclusion that Angola might consider a partial withdrawal (2/3 of the total number) within a specified period (2 years), the remaining 1/3 being stationed in Northern Angola. In return, the US would recognise the Luanda government, South Africa would withdraw *all* its troops from *Angola*, terminate aid to UNITA and accept forthwith the application of Resolution 435, which also implies, of course, withdrawal of their troops from *Namibia.* What is the real situation? Fact-finding may assist in producing sufficient clarity to allow a proper assessment of the facts.

(E) Agreement and controversy: the interested parties

Agreed issues

To recapitulate on the points of agreement:

(a) The parties agree that independence *must* be granted to Namibia in accordance with Resolution 435.
(b) They agree that a New Constitution must be elaborated by a freely elected Constituent Assembly and that Namibia will be a 'unitary, sovereign and democratic state.'
(c) They agree in principle that a cease-fire agreement is an

essential pre-condition for implementation of Resolution 435.

(d) All parties share the view that *all* foreign troops should depart — although not necessarily all simultaneously. (All parties also accept the fact that in due course constructive arrangements are to be negotiated for maintaining active economic relations with South Africa, after independence).

These agreed issues cover important steps toward independence. They form a good basis for further discussions and progress.

Controversial issues

The major issues on which there is still a large area of disagreement between the parties are:

(a) Departure of Cuban and South-African troops: when and under what conditions? This question is *the* stumbling block in the discussion.
(b) Timing of the implementation of Resolution 435: *Immediately* or *after consultation* between the Namibian parties?
(c) *Details* of a cease-fire agreement before implementing Resolution 435.

Attitudes of the parties

What are the prospects of removing these obstacles by mediation, or indeed by other means?

As a generalization, borne out by long experience, the most important factor in the success or failure of a mediation is the attitude of the parties themselves:

— do they sincerely want to resolve the issue?
— are they prepared to compromise to reach agreement?
— will they negotiate in good faith, not imputing bad faith to their opponents and acting honestly themselves?

— will they refrain from actions which may aggravate the situation so as to endanger the outcome of the mediation (can an indefinite cease-fire be made to hold?; will unilateral constitutional changes in Namibia be abandoned?)?
— if complete success is not achieved quickly, will they be willing to continue the attempt to make some progress?

In the light of past events it would be foolish to make any assumptions on these ponts. Before proceeding to mediation, patient probing to establish the parties' attitudes, face-to-face, through third parties and by any other means possible, would be essential, but for the present purpose let us leave this vital question open and proceed to consider the next steps.

The parties

In this instance, it is not immediately obvious who would be 'the parties' to a mediation. Who are the parties with an 'interest' in the outcome?

(a) The Republic of South Africa:
   South Africa obviously is a party having ruled Namibia since 1915 and acted since 1920 as mandatory power exercising sovereign functions.

(b) The people of Namibia:
   — SWAPO (the South West African People's Organization)
   This is the main liberation movement of Namibia, which has been fighting for independence since the late 1960s and is shouldering the major burden of the armed struggle against South Africa's rule in Namibia. Some of their centers of action are located *outside* Namibia (mainly in Angola), from where they direct their activities and incursions into Namibia. They are recognized by the UN as 'sole and authentic representative' of Namibia.

   — Other Namibian parties and organizations:
   There are about 1.1—1.2 million Namibians *in* Namibia (out

of a total of around 1.3 million), whose destiny is at stake. They all or nearly all, stand for total independence, but their voice has not always been heard. The internal parties speak for some, and SWAPO speaks for some, but not necessarily all. So far, SWAPO has understandably resisted South African proposals for additional internal participants, but would it be sensible to launch a mediation without some broadening of Namibian representation? Will SWAPO be willing to take an initiative to this end?

(c) The Frontline States:

The six states Tanzania, Mozambique, Zambia, Botswana, Zimbabwe and Angola have rendered active support to the cause of Namibian independence for many years and have advocated it without fail in the UN and in other international forums. Being neighboring States of, or otherwise close to, Namibia, their voice is of some weight in any Namibian settlement.

(d) Western Contact Group:

This group, which (similar to the frontline states) has no legal standing, formed itself in 1977 and consists of the USA, UK, Canada, France and West Germany, the five western countries who were members of the Security Council in 1978. The group, under American leadership, has held many meetings with South Africa, SWAPO and also Angola, to find a solution for the Namibian question. They made considerable progress, but without reaching the final goal and their efforts have now run into the ground.

(e) The United Nations:

The UN position, and its direct and indirect roles, have been discussed earlier. (See Chapter B4).

These six parties are particularly involved in, and committed to Namibian independence and have thus an interest in the handling of the problems, although at two basically different levels:

— South Africa and the Namibian people (SWAPO and others) are

the genuine, directly concerned players in the game, who can 'make or break' Namibia's independence.
— The six frontline states, the Western Contact Group and the UN itself are parties who can play a helpful hand in a settlement and who have already produced many efforts to that end, although distinct from each other and not always in harmony.

While it would be advisable for all these interests to be formally associated with a mediation, a distinction would have to be made between the two groups to reflect the relative strength of their concerns.

In addition, the guerrilla movement UNITA in Angola has demanded to be allowed to participate in coalition talks in Angola and in negotiations for Namibian independence. The author's opinion is that UNITA represents a domestic Angolan problem to be handled by Angolans. There are no convincing arguments why UNITA should become a party in a Namibian settlement.

(F) Procedural alternatives for a settlement

Mediation by the UN?

Article 33 of the UN Charter provides for the possibility of mediation by the UN. The question that first has to be decided is whether, in order to reach Namibian independence, the mediation should go through the UN or whether other alternatives might be explored.

Resolution 435 is a UN Security Council Resolution and the responsibility for its enforcement would normally fall on the UN, i.e., on the Secretary-General, who in turn keeps the Security Council abreast of events. The pattern which evolved from this procedure represents a well-tested and forceful procedure. With a UN Resolution as backing, a mediation exercise is stronger and more authoritative than other procedures, but it is also more political. The decisive strength is undivided backing by the Security Council, the firm authority of the Secretary-General, the material assistance of the UN and the expertise available.

In the view of the author of this paper, the extremely delicate and politically sensitive nature of the Namibian exercise imposes the need for the utmost discretion in the handling of the issues at stake. Discretion is of the essence; progress on substantial aspects can be achieved only in repose and quietude, without potentially damaging publicity which raises wrong hopes, opens the door to outside pressures and renders concessions by one or the other of the parties more difficult. The Namibian exercise falls clearly into this category. This does not imply that mediation should take place without the UN, not at all. It simply means that the UN organs cannot handle all mediation cases in the same way, passing information to the Security Council on the progress or lack of it all the time. Neither the Secretary-General, nor the mediator should be asked to give *full* and public information (except on procedural progress) at regular intervals to UN bodies and thus indirectly to the whole world. This might, on occasion, have adverse consequences on the course of the exercise, particularly if one of the parties already entertains reservations against a UN involvement in the mediation. While the UN could not remain aloof from any fresh mediatory effort, it might well be wise for the UN to play a background role after being instrumental in setting up a mediation.

What really matters in such an exercise is, above all, a satisfactory *outcome* for the parties. Of much less relevance is the fact whether a satisfactory settlement has been reached 'by the UN' or by travelling a slightly different road.

The writer of this paper is in no doubt that whatever path is ultimately chosen, the legitimate interest of the Security Council in a peaceful solution of the conflict and in an adequate flow of information can be met without jeopardizing whatever modest chances of success a mediation might have.

The parties' choice of alternative procedures

Any procedure chosen for dealing with the Namibian question must be approved by clear consent of the parties. Such consent is indispensable; it must be evident that the parties have the genuine *political will* for a settlement and the readiness for honest cooperation to that end.

This political will has to be determined with *no ambiguity whatever* at the very beginning of the search for an arrangement.

Two of the 'interested parties' (see above) have already played the role of intermediary, but not at the explicit request of the main protagonists. Could they be called upon again at the present juncture?

(a) *The Western Contact Group*

The Western Contact Group has been at work for 8 years; it was formed in 1977. In recent periods, its mandate was carried forward mostly by the USA, whereas the other members took a back seat. The USA plays the major role by direct involvement: by means of its relationship with South Africa, its contacts with SWAPO and other Namibian parties, the hoped-for recognition of the Angolan government, the aid-package for Angola and Namibia, and above all by the demand for Cuban withdrawal.

A 'Big Power-State' as intermediary, as mediator, may, in specific cases, be the right choice because of the trump cards they can play.

The problematic side of this particular procedure is that a Big Power is a *political* authority and weighs possible solutions from the angle of its own political viewpoint. The East-West military competition may be brought into consideration. This is not desirable, neither in Namibia, nor elsewhere.

Still, the USA's role and its impact on an overall Namibian settlement are such that they must be deemed to constitute a partner in the discussions, because of the Cuban troops question. But a procedure under the guidance of the Western Contact Group or the USA would be problematic because it would be too political. It would meet with reservations in African countries and in the Security Council. It is also quite likely that the USA would not even wish to assume such a mandate.

(b) *The Frontline States*

Another group which has been dealing with Namibia for years is that of the six 'Frontline States'. Their position on South Africa is well-known and so is their relationship with SWAPO and Angola, and their relationship with South Africa. The views which they have expressed in the past on the Namibian case are quite firm and do not allow much room for any degree of flexibility. This strongly established attitude is unlikely to qualify the 'Front-liners' as a mediator acceptable to all parties. They are a party themselves.

Like the USA, therefore, they cannot be considered for the role of mediator, for the time being.

(c) *Arbitration/International Court of Justice — Commission of Enquiry*

Besides mediation, other modes of settling international disputes are:
— arbitration
— International Court of Justice
— Commission of Enquiry

These three methods, tested in many other areas, are unsuitable in the case of Namibia's independence because it is a political issue. 'Arbitration' constitutes a final, binding verdict, without negotiations and without recourse to an appeal. Such a procedure is not suited for a *political* dispute; moreover, it is difficult to see that it would meet with the approval of the parties, as it does not provide for any opportunity to negotiate about, or modify the verdict.

The 'International Court of Justice' is equally unsuited for judging the Namibian case. The Court is a *legal* body; it has to apply recognized *legal* rules to established facts; neither compromise nor negotiation over its ruling falls within its province. The Court acts outside of political issues. As has been shown above, earlier references to the International Court have, regrettably, not had much influence on the course of events.

Still another way of tackling disputes is a 'Commission of Enquiry', which, according to its mandate, has to scrutinize the facts of a case, without coming to political or other conclusions or submitting recommendations. In order to settle a dispute, however, a position must be taken; settlement usually takes place on the basis of recommendations or proposals, on which the parties negotiate; theirs is the right to seek compromises, if that meets the views of the parties. A 'Commission of Enquiry' thus also appears to be out of the question for the Namibian conflict.

Classical mediation

The remaining and, in our opinion, best suited settlement strategy is the classical mediation between the parties. It has several attributes that make this mode palatable as a practical and equitable process for dealing with a political dispute:

— The mediator does not represent any party; he is totally impartial and neutral.
— The mediation presupposes objective fact-finding. It is part of the mediator's task to undertake it.
— He is free to take his own initiatives to arrive at reliable fact-finding.
— A mediation mandate implies the right and obligation of the mediator to submit recommendations (in the light of needs which arise *during* the exercise or, comprehensively, at the conclusion of it).
— In agreeing to mediation, the parties agree to discuss the mediator's proposals as a possible negotiating basis.
— The parties keep the privilege to accept, reject or modify the recommendations in the negotiations which are an essential part in a mediation. Theirs is the last word.
— The mediator gives his assistance, if so requested, in the negotiations to find an ultimate solution.
— Mediation always leaves room for compromise among the parties.

Also important is the fact that an impartial mediator may be a means of de-politicizing a highly delicate political question and bringing it back to its true, cold and sober dimension. He is immune to political influences, while he retains the right to consult any advisory body of his selection, whether directly involved or not. The door for seeking outside views and for measuring one's own conclusions against those of outsiders remains open for him — everywhere and at any time and at any place.

(G) Setting-up a Namibian Mediation exercise

(These rules apply to any mediation exercise, whether within the framework of the UN or not.)

Some rules of the game exist which are the result of practical experience and which should be observed in setting up a concrete mediation exercise.

(a) A list of potential mediators (a government, an international institution, individual personalities) should be submitted to the parties, preferably 8—10 names, from which the directly involved countries select a mediator, by unanimous designation.

(In a specific case known to the writer, 10 names were submitted from which each of the several governments involved were asked to select three potential mediators. If *one* and the same name appeared in all selections, he was chosen as the man to carry out the mandate).

(b) This list of names can be established by the UN Secretary-General, by the Secretary-General of the OAU, by the Frontline States, by the Western Contact Group, by non-official organizations (for instance, the Carnegie Endowment for International Peace), perhaps also by an authority of international standing. The right of *final selection* is vested in the parties in the dispute. In the case of lack of agreement, the President of the OAU or of the International Court of Justice can be entrusted with the authority to make the choice.

In the Namibian case, a *joint* proposal for a mediator list by the UN Secretary-General and the Secretary-General of the OAU might be a promising procedure for a mediation exercise in Africa.

(c) The next step, a crucial one, is to define the issues clearly and dispassionately, and to agree upon the mediator's terms of reference. This difficult task should be undertaken jointly by the main parties (South Africa and Namibia) and the mediator possibly with active advice from the authority which set up the mediation. The other 'interested parties' would also need to be consulted and to accept the terms of reference.

The main points still in controversy on the implementation of Resolution 435 have been set out above, i.e.:
  — the Cuban link;
  — timing (before or after discussions including SWAPO and other Namibian parties and organizations);
  — details of the cease-fire arrangements.

It is clear that the formulation of these issues into mutually acceptable terms of reference would in itself be an exercise in diplomacy.

Bearing in mind that the purpose of a mediation would be to accelerate, not delay, implementation of the settlement proposals, it should also be considered:

— whether there are points in the settlement plan or constitutional principles which need to be argued out more fully before proceeding (e.g., the steps between the conclusion of the Constituent Assembly's business and the installation of an independent government receive scant attention in the settlement plan; this is quite likely to be a deliberate choice on the part of the Contact Group, but the parties cannot disregard them and need to *work together* for a smooth transition).

— whether there are practical problems (e.g., on the timing or sequence of steps in the 435 process) which need review because of the lapse of time or any further negotiation for any reason?

— what sort of start might be made in advance of overall agreement (e.g., release of political prisoners and detainees; an end of conscription in Namibia — conscription is a sharply divisive element; what more can be done by agreement in advance of independence to localize the civil administration?).

Any of these matters, in addition to the three main issues still unresolved might figure in the terms of reference.

(d) The mediator's independence must be fully recognized and respected. The responsibility for his work and his recommendations are *his alone*. But he will be well advised to seek counsel and guidance (not instructions!) from other sources, whenever he deems this justified. However, any advice or counsel from outside can never dilute his own, undoubted responsibility for his activity.

(e) Duration of the exercise? The politically sensitive Namibian mediation may take up to 2—4 years or even more. The mediator must therefore be prepared to be burdened with a mandate of some length.

A time-limit for the full mediation is not indicated, but the mediator should report at the latest *one year after starting* his work, whether he meets with sufficient political will by the parties or whether the exercise is a 'non-starter'. In the latter case, he may elect to return his mandate by giving public reasons for it.

(f) Supporting staff: will be selected by the mediator, not by the parties. Their loyalty and responsibility go unequivocally to the mediator.

(g) Budgetary matters: The funds required for the exercise have to be determined in the light of yearly budgets by the mediator. Assurance is to be given that sufficient funds will be provided, on a yearly basis, for at least two years, with the need for flexibility and willingness for replenishment after two years, if justified. The funds might come from governmental or non-governmental bodies (for example, the International Peace Foundations).

(h) The mediator has to address regular interim reports to the parties, say every four months, on the progress of his work, without detailing the substance of controversial issues. A copy of these reports will be sent to those offices as designated by the parties.

(i) If the Namibian mediation is to be handled by agreement among the parties as 'a mediation by the UN', then appropriate arrangements will have to be worked out between the UN Secretary-General and the mediator which correspond to the Secretary-General's requirements, while at the same time recognizing the mediator's responsibility and independence. This must take into account the mediator's duty to fully respect the rules of discretion and confidentiality, whenever the circumstances of his work so require.

(k) Finally, the mediator should remain available, if the parties so request, to give assistance in the negotiations about a settlement and thereafter when a Constituent Assembly is drafting a new Namibian Constitution.

APOCALYPSE NOW: THE CHURCHES AND REVOLUTION IN SOUTH AFRICA

Burgess Carr
International Consultant on Human and Ethical Issues in African Development

The award of the Nobel Peace Prize in 1984 to Bishop Desmond Tutu was unprecedented in at least two respects: it was the second time that the Prize had been awarded to an African. Another South African, Chief Albert Lutuli was awarded the Prize in 1960 in recognition of his role in resisting apartheid. In the case of Bishop Tutu, the Nobel Committee cited his leading role as general secretary of the South African Council of Churches (SACC) in the struggle against apartheid. Thus world attention has been focused on the role of the Churches in the struggle for peace and justice in South Africa.

It is also significant that the SACC was chosen for this outstanding recognition. The SACC is the ecumenical affiliate in South Africa of the World Council of Churches and the All Africa Conference of Churches, and as such it has been subjected to the most intense harassment by the South African authorities. In 1981 the 'Eloff Commission' was appointed to investigate the affairs of the Council. The Commission heard testimony from the head of the South African State Security, who suggested that the Council be either banned or declared an 'affected organization'. What the award of the Nobel Peace Prize to the general secretary of the SACC did in effect was to bring about a change of places between the SACC and the South African government. Five years ago, it was the South African Council of Churches that was the victim of reproach and on trial for its very existence. Today, it is the whole evil system of apartheid that is universally unmasked and denounced as constituting the major threat to peace and justice, not only within South Africa, but throughout Southern

Africa, and beyond. Therefore, new expectations have been raised with respect to the future role of the Churches in achieving liberation and reconciliation in South Africa. The purpose of this essay is to analyze certain major factors in determining whether and how those expectations might be fulfilled.

The Enigma

Unlike the uprising of Sharpeville (1960) and Soweto (1976), the political unrest and violence unleashed in September 1984 have not abated; rather, they have become endemic. South Africa has moved from the perimeter and become the epicenter of global racial conflict. With more than eleven hundred deaths over an eighteen months period, civil war looms on the horizon, and the apartheid regime maintains itself solely by its formidable capacity for violence. There is increased concern, even alarm, in every quarter: in corporate boardrooms, in the banking industry, universities, national and local legislative bodies, and, yes, the churches. The media brings Bishop Tutu into suburban bedrooms around the world, where people hear him compare apartheid with Nazism; call for economic pressure and disinvestment; and hypothesize that the apartheid regime would probably use its tactical nuclear weapons to destroy his beautiful country before they would agree to share power with the African majority. A direful scenario indeed.

However, it is when one hears the Bishop say solemnly, 'If I were a young black South African, I would not listen to Desmond Tutu,' that one can begin to recognize the frustration discernible in the tragic interplay between despair and enigma. To gain insight into the enigma, it is necessary to understand how political mythology in South Africa nurtures and legitimizes the racist paradigm which governs and regulates every aspect of life in that society.

Political mythology in South African can be summarized under three types:

(a) myths concerning the *vacant land*, the *unassimilability of cultures*, and the *ten black nations*;

(b) *anti-imperialist myths* constructed as part of the Afrikaner reaction against British imperialism in the late nineteenth century, and

(c) *religious myths* that portray the Afrikaner as a 'Chosen People' with a God-given mission to rule South Africa.

It is the argument of this essay that while the political and economic significance of apartheid cannot be ignored, the feature of the South African reality which is more basic than either and which actually provides apartheid with its final justification is Afrikaner religion. The emergence of fundamentalist religious revolutions in many parts of the world has begun to erode some of the secular bias of the West in interpreting the values and norms of modern societies. In the case of South Africa, the moral fervor and idealism, the devotion and commitment which drives Africa's most technologically advanced nation are deeply rooted in values that are resolutely religious.

According to Leonard Thompson, the authorative South African historian at Yale, *The Covenant* has been far the most influential component of the Afrikaner political mythology ever since the birth of the nationalist movement in the late nineteenth century. The core of the myth can be traced to the battle of Blood River on 16 December 1838 when an emigrant commando commanded by Andries Pretorius, armed with guns and cannons, and, aided by about 'sixty African allies' defeated the Zulu army of some ten thousand strong. The chronicler of the battle was a young colored secretary to Pretorius named Jan Bantjes. Bantjes wrote that 'the commando was inspired by profound religious fervor. All the officers were extremely solicitious of the favor of God. They held prayer meetings every day.'

The crucial religious event occured on Sunday, 9 December.

'That Sunday morning before the service began, the Chief Commandant called together the men who would conduct the service and asked them to suggest to the congregation that they should all pray to God fervently in spirit and in truth for his help and assistance in the struggle with the enemy; (he said) that he wanted to make a vow to the Almighty, (if they were willing), that "should the Lord give us the victory, we would raise a House to the memory of His Great Name, wherever it shall please Him;'' and that they should also invoke the aid and assistance of God to enable them to fulfill this vow; and that we should note the day of the victory in a book, to make it known even to our latest posterity, so that it might be celebrated to the Honor of God.'

Bantjes reported that those responsible for leading the worship service 'were glad to hear it' and led by Sarel Cilliers, who had been a Church elder in the colony, they proceeded to make generous use of the Old Testament Scriptures e.g., Psalms 38:12—16, and Judges 6:1—24.

A week after the Battle, on 23 December, Pretorius wrote the following in the first paragraph of his own report of the battle:

'The undertaking was great and our force small, as it consisted of only 460 men; therefore we could entertain no confidence than in the justness of our cause and in the God of our Fathers; and the result thus far has also shown that —
He who trust in the good God
Has surely not built on sand.'

And he concluded with this statement about the *Vow*:

'I wish to inform you that we have here decided among ourselves *to make known* the day of our victory, being *Sunday, the 16th day of this month of December, among our entire community*, and that we shall consecrate it to the Lord, and celebrate it with Thanksgivings, since, before we fought against the enemy, we *promised in a public prayer* that should we manage to win the victory, we would build a house to the Lord in memory of his name, wherever He shall indicate it; which vow we now also hope to honor, with the help of the Lord, now that he has blessed us and heard our prayers.'

The *Voortrekkers* (as the emigrants were called) failed to honor the *Vow* and it fell into 'rapid oblivion' until the 1880s, when Afrikaner clergy began to assert the claim that the *Voortrekkers* were a 'Chosen People' and drew parallels between their own history and that of the biblical Israel. Thus the *Covenant* became the prime symbol of Afrikaner Christianity and culture, and the supreme vindication of Afrikaner hegemony in South Africa. One of the first acts of the Union Parliament in 1910 was to make the anniversary of the battle of Blood River a public holiday. Following the victory of the National Party in 1948, Afrikaner cultural leaders crystallized, popularized and nationalized the myth of the Covenant. The dedication of the Voortrekker Monument on 16 December 1949, has turned that date into the greatest ethnic event in the Afrikaner calendar, with features identical to the racist ideology in Nazi Germany, appealing to the individual's need for organic community and for the shelter of a firm and established morality.

In South Africa, more than in any other Protestant country, the clergy, and particularly those of Dutch Reformed Churches, (DRCs) are a major force in politics. D.F. Malan, who led the National Party to victory on the *apartheid* platform was a clergyman; so was the thoroughly racist brother of former Prime Minister John Vorster, and so also is Andries Treurnicht, who led the recent Conservative breakaway from the National Party. The principal Dutch Reformed Church in South Africa is the Nederduitse Gereformeerde Kerk (NGK). As described by Dr. John de Gruchy of the University of Capetown, the NGK,

'with its million-and-a-half white members is quite clearly the dominant Church in terms of its access to the policy makers of the nation. Included within its ranks are most of the members of Parliament and of the provincial councils. Its members virtually control many of the town councils throughout the land. The vast majority of people employed by the government in various capacities and institutions, including the police and military, belong to the DRC (i.e., the NGK).'

As might be expected, the NGK consistently adopts a conservative approach to the politics of the apartheid regime. As such, it is riddled with contradictions. It interprets Scripture as upholding the essential unity of humankind, but claims also that ethnic diversity accords with the will of God; it rejects racial injustice and discrimination in principle, but accepts the policy of 'separate development.'

To the right of the NGK is the Nederduitsch Hervormde Kerk (NHK) which is still more rigidly and unanimously conservative; while to the left is the small Gereformeerde Kerk van Suid Afrika (GKSA) which has produced some dissent that is of no political significance. This pervasive conservatism has alienated the Afrikaans Churches from the rest of institutional Christianity, both within South Africa and abroad.

Conservative observers, largely Protestant and evangelical have found it impossible to distance themselves theologically from the Afrikaner's Calvinism. On the other hand, the emergence of liberation theologies in the Third World and in Protestant ecumenical circles, including those in South Africa, are consistently sharply critical of apartheid. However, the controlling hermeneutic employed by liberation theologians rests on the same assumptions used by conservative opponents. The God of the Bible is understood to be engaged in repeating his historic adventures with biblical Israel, save that now Israel is no longer Jewish. In the new view, Israel consists of a non-Jewish elect: either Calvinists covenanted to uphold the infallibility of the Bible (the conservatives view) or the politically and culturally oppressed, whoever they may be. In a word, the major religious interpretations of the plight of South Africa today are redactions of Calvinism which hold that the pre-exilic history of Israel is recapitulated in the Afrikaners' struggle for freedom, first from British imperialism and now from the onslaught of Black ('Bantu') hostility and communism. This is the view of the conservative Afrikaner. The liberation theologians on the theological left believe *pari passu* that Israel's history is about to be repeated in the struggle of Africans for freedom from their white oppressors in league with international capitalism.

In this context, the usages of apocalyptic imagery to identify the righteousness of one's cause are ominous indeed. As the polarization in South Africa sharpens, the rhetoric on both sides begin to sound as if people are preparing for the final apocalyptic battle between good and eveil. Speaking on the Day of the Vow in 1983, a conservative DRC clergyman told a gathering in the Cape Town suburb of Rodenbosch;

'Discrimination, injustice and suffering will always exist until

Christ comes again, and then Christ will remove them. Through fighting against discrimination now, people are trying to take God's task over from Him, and thus open the way for *the Antichrist*. He who wants to do more than what God wants him to do, commits suicide, as will happen to the United Nations and the world powers.'

Such an exposition of 'racist theology' must inevitably provoke a response, and that has come swiftly in the *Kairos Document* (KD) issued by 151 South African church leaders representing Roman Catholics, 'mainline' protestant, 'evangelical' protestant, men and women, clergy and lay. Five of the signatories are members of the NGK. The Document, entitled 'Challenge to the Church' is sub-titled, 'Theological Comment on the Political Crisis in South Africa.' It is helpful to look at this document which many have called South Africa's *Barmen Declaration*. (A watershed document in the history of the modern church, the Barmen Declaration issued in 1934 by Dietrich Bonhoeffer and other leaders of the Confessing Church rejected the efforts of the Nazi state to co-opt the church. Above all, it decried the readiness of church members and movements to be seduced by Hitler's nationalism, racism and militarism.)

The *Kairos Document* denounces the official 'State Theology' by citing the blasphemous use of God's holy name in the preamble to the new apartheid constitution:

'In humble submission to Almighty God, who controls the destinies of nations and the history of peoples; who gathered our forebears together from many lands and gave them this their own; who has guided them from generation to generation; who has wondrously delivered them from the dangers that beset them. . . .'

The KD finds this 'state theology' is heretical:

'This god is an idol. It is as mischievous, sinister and evil as any of the idols that the prophets of Israel had to contend with. Here we have a god who is historically on the side of the white settlers, who dispossessed black people of their land and who gives the major part of the land to his 'chosen people.' It is the god of superior weapons who conquered those who were armed with nothing but spears. It is the god of the casspirs and hippos, the god of teargas and rubber bullets, sjamboks, prison cells and death sentences. Here is the God who exalts the proud and humbles the poor — the very opposite of the God of the Bible who 'scatters the proud of heart, pulls down the mighty from their thrones and exalts the humble' (Luke 1:51—52). From a theological point of view the opposite of God in the Bible is the devil, Satan. The god of the South African State is not merely an idol or false god, it is the devil disguised as Almighty God — *the antichrist.'*

Clearly, both the religious views of the DRC and the KD cannot be correct, even though both appeal to the same biblical sources. Yet, since both take religion so seriously, they can at least be said to reflect the fundamental enigma of South Africa: it is a religious society which secular critics cannot comprehend unless they are prepared to take a people's religious commitment seriously. And South Africa is a religious society which many even in the Churches cannot understand because of their own exclusivist theological commitments, left and right. This is evident in the claims and counter claims about whose side God is on, and indeed, whether God is really God, or the 'Antichrist.'

The Kairos Document has a pedigree. Over sixty years ago, J.H. Oldham, father of the modern ecumenical movement, wrote in *Christianity and the Race Problem*:

'Christianity is not primarily a philosophy, but a crusade. As Christ was sent by the Father, so He sends His disciples *to set up in the world* the Kingdom of God. His coming is a declaration of war — a *war to the death* against the powers of the devil. He was manifested to destroy the works of the devil. Hence when Christians find in the world a state of things that are not in accord with the truth which they have learned from Christ, *their concern is not that it should be explained, but that it should be ended*. In that temper we must approach everything in the relations between races. . . .'

The KD is the most recent attempt by the Christian inside South Africa to take up Oldham's challenge. As early as 1948, the non-Dutch Reformed Churches in South Africa issues statements criticizing apartheid, but their practices fell far short of their rhetoric. If it now looks as though the situation in South Africa has reached apocalyptic dimensions, then the events in the period between 1960 to 1977 might well have been the prologue. At center stage in this prologue was the Christian Institute, led by Beyers Naude, Bishop Tutu's successor as general secretary of the South African Council of Churches.

The Prologue — Sharpeville to Soweto

Sharpeville (1960) was a judgment call against the churches. Sixty-seven (67) unarmed passive resisters demonstrating against the Pass Laws were shot to death by the South African police. The Government responding to its own violence banned the African National Congress (ANC) and the Pan Africanist Congress (PAC). The English-speaking Churches, not unlike their DRC counterparts were apathetic, prefering to concentrate on personal salvation, emphasizing charity to the neglect of justice, and willing to place the Kingdom of God, not in this world, but outside history.

In response to the Sharpeville massacre, the World Council of Churches (WCC) sought to play a mediating role by convening an international, ecumenical and interracial conference at Cottesloe. By Oldham's standards, the Cottesloe statements were modest. They declared that no Christian should be excluded from any church on racial grounds; all racial groups should share in the responsibilities, rewards and privileges of society; there were no scriptural grounds for denial of mixed marriages, and that all persons had the right to own land where they lived. Chief Albert Luthuli expressed cautious support for the document, stating that the message must be given some practical effect. He suggested that it was not too late for white Christians to look at the Gospels and redefine their allegiance. . . . Time was running out.

The backlash in the DRCs and among the Afrikaner community was swift and severe. Dr. Verwoerd, the Prime Minister, other

Nationalist politicians and conservative clergy brought strong pressure through the state, the church and the press to bear on the synods of the NGK in order to make them reject Cottesloe. The synods called for major revisions of the Cottesloe consensus, and when these were not forthcoming, the three Dutch Reformed Churches withdrew from membership in the World Council of Churches.

The Christian Institute (CI) was organized by Beyers Naude, and a few others who were at Cottesloe, in order to continue the task of deepening the Churches understanding of the Gospel demand for justice as a constitutive element of their mission *in this world*. In practical terms, this amounted to little more than charity and paternalism. Whites were called upon to make small sacrifices in the hope that moral suasion would impress the regime. Blacks were insulted by this approach. For half a century, they had engaged in non-violent persuasion and reached the conclusion that the root of South Africa's problem was the 'bankruptcy of compassion toward the underprivileged.'

In the 1970s, the CI sought to respond to black pressures for social and political reform. The CI committed itself to working with the victims of repression and supporting black initiatives for justice and black vision of the future of South Africa. This strategy of working for black majority rule a new economic and political order in South Africa generated tensions in the multiracial churches. At the same time, organizations advocating black solidarity were bringing increased pressure to bear on the churches and ecumenical agencies like the CI and the South African Council of Churches (SACC).

The SACC 'Message to the People of South Africa' in 1968 coincided with the publication of the first report of the CI's Study Project on Christianity in an Apartheid Society (Spro-Cas). The report declared Apartheid to be in total contradiction to the Gospel, relying on the 'maintenance of White supremacy,' and 'rooted in sin.' The *Message* of the SACC described Apartheid as a 'false offer of salvation' that is 'hostile to Christianity,' and said that the 'policy of racial separation must ultimately require that the Church should cease to be the Church.' At that time and in that context, these were bold statements, but their effect on White society was minimal. Only the Government seemed to take notice.

The Minister of Police warned the CI against 'causing people to feel guilty' and after a period of intense harassment, during which many whites associated with the CI fled the country, the CI was declared unlawful. Beyers Naude, a former moderator of the NGK and member of the Broederbond (the Afrikaner secret society) was banned. Attempts by the prime minister, John Vorster, to compel the multiracial Churches to withdraw from the WCC in the wake of the grants from its Program to Combat Racism to the liberation movements were resisted by both the SACC and the member Churches.

And well they might, for as repression of blacks intensified at every level, the 70s saw the emergence of the 'Black Consciousness' Movement. Young Black leaders recognized the failure of the Churches resulting from their willingness to *confront* the apartheid state. Churches became more and more racially polarized as strikes and violent confrontations became common occurrences. In 1973, Spro-Cas II, entitled *A Taste of Power*, explicitly called for an equal sharing of political rights, and removal of discriminatory laws and practices. But on the whole the Churches still failed to act.

The reason for this failure had primarily to do with the paralysis resulting from the violence/non-violence debate which followed the WCC grants to the liberation movements. The controversy over violence came to supercede all the other promising issues that were emerging at several levels in the South African churches. It was a lopsided debate, however; since the violence question had been settled for most blacks by the repression of the 50s and the massacres of the 60s. Blacks saw the debate about violence as a technique for avoiding the real issues. Consequently, they formed their own organizations like the South African Students Organization (SASO) and made a clear break from white liberals.

SASO was a black organization — 'black' being interpreted to mean those who were legally and traditionally discriminated against and oppressed politically, economically and socially. Being Black was not a pigmentation, but rather a reflection of mental attitude. Thus the ideological basis for movements like the Student Coordinating Committee that directed the Soweto uprisings, and even the school and rent boycotts, and township riots now taking place were put into place.

Beyond Soweto — Apocalypse

The banning of the Christian Institute in 1977, following the Soweto uprising of 1976, was a fitting requiem for the past dispensation of church resolutions, consultations and paternalistic programs initiated and controlled by white liberals. They were all part of the prologue to the coming apocalypse — the confrontation with the 'Antichrist.' Time has run out. Now is the time.

That is the message of the *Kairos Document*:

> 'The time has come. The moment of truth has arrived. South Africa has been plunged into a crisis that is shaking the foundations and there is every indication that the crisis has only just begun. . . It is the Kairos or moment of truth not only for apartheid but also for the Church.'

The KD is critical of the 'State Theology' developed by the DRCs to legitimize the poltical mythology that energizes the racist paradigm in South Africa. It is equally brutal in exposing the inadequacies of 'Church Theology' in the English-speaking churches who have provided the script for the prologue to the apocalypse. And it dares to suggest the outline of a 'Prophetic Theology' that gives adequate and appropriate attention to social analysis, does combat with oppression, exposes the immorality and illigitimacy of tyranny and offers a new basis for hope; one that does not rely upon the oppressor.

KD challenges its readers to *action*, reminding them that only participants earn the right to be prophets. Obviously the individual must decide for oneself what action he/she will engage in, but the orientation is clear — only the particulars are left to choice.

KD is a document of enormous force precisely because it offers a clearly articulated message appropriate to apocalyptic times. And because it is being shaped in the flames of violent upheavals, it has an authenticity and integrity that no word from any Church in South Africa can claim. It could well be 'the Word of the Lord.'

The KD makes it clear that what's happening in South Africa is no longer an *anti-apartheid* struggle but a *pro-liberation* struggle. Perhaps that is the reason why Afrikaner leaders including the

State President, P.W. Botha is now publically declaring that he is against apartheid. Apartheid is no longer the issue; liberation is.

Consequently, the document offers insights that clarify several significant aspects of the liberation struggle for peace and justice in South Africa. The KD reminds us that it is a *violent* struggle: the systemic violence of apartheid, and the counter-violence of resistence.

The apartheid regime continues to suppress peaceful protest by violence and even carries out frequent attacks against neighboring independent states.

The KD makes clear that what is going on in South Africa is a *national* liberation struggle. The momentum for the struggle arises from the people. As successive generations of leaders are killed, imprisoned, banned or exiled, new leadership emerges from the people.

Thirdly, it is a *revolutionary* struggle which is taking place in South Africa. Reform is no longer an option. The apartheid system is demonized and must be dismantled. It cannot be reformed.

Finally, the KD offers a new way of identifying the Church in South Africa. It reveals that there are really two Churches: The *institutional* Church and the people's Church. The latter are drawn together, not by doctrinal, racial or class commonalities, but by a commitment to the liberation struggle. It is they who offer reason to hope that after liberation, reconciliation and peace will come speedily.

Note on the author: Burgess Carr, a native of Liberia, was formerly general secretary of the All Africa Conference of Churches.

MEDIA AND CHANGE IN SOUTH AFRICA

Julie Frederikse
Southern Africa correspondent for US National Public Radio, Harare

On a sunny Friday afternoon in surburban Pretoria in January 1980, three armed members of the African National Congress burst into the Silverton branch of a major Afrikaner-owned bank and took hostage all the staff and customers. Six hours later, a South African Police counterinsurgency unit stormed the bank. The three black guerrillas and two white hostages were killed. The other casualty — which went unreported in the blaze of publicity surrounding the siege — was truth.

News reports on the event were censored according to the Inquests Act (implemented after the international media focus on the probe into the 1977 death in police custody of Black Consciousness leader Steve Biko) and the Police Act, which requires newspapers to prove in a court of law that reports on police matters are true or face a five-year prison sentence or a R 10,000 fine. An expurgated account, published in a media journal some months later,[1] reveals clearly what the government's censors wanted to hide. 'Among the guerrilla demands', begins the reporter's second paragraph, 'was... BLANK'. The rest of the sentence, detailing facts reported everywhere else in the world except South Africa, that the guerrillas had demanded the release from prison of Nelson Mandela and other ANC leaders, was blanked out. Press interviews with the freed hostages — 'the terrorists told us they were freedom fighters and interested in equal rights, not money' — were suppressed. The South African public, through the media, was simply told that the guerrillas' demands were not political and that the police felt that to publicize them would be 'tactically incorrect'.

Reporters, photographers and TV crews who had been denied access to the bank throughout the siege were, *after* the bloodshed, ushered into what looked like a floodlit movie set to graphically document the gory defeat of the 'terrorists'. Only one newspaper in South Africa, a black daily subsequently banned, referred to the gunmen as 'guerrillas'. Few papers highlighted the selection of the Volkskas Bank as a target: 'because it is the bank of the Afrikaner nation and they are the oppressors', as explained by one guerrilla to a hostage. Not a single media report dared to speculate about the wisdom of the authorities' handling of the incident, and the completely unsubstantiated police version of the death of the two women hostages — that they were killed by the dead guerrillas and not by police bullets — remained unquestioned. Moreover, the implications of the ANC's contention that the guerrillas had acted without authorization were never publicly analyzed in South Africa; in fact, it later emeged that South African intelligence agents had produced a fake ANC press statement claiming responsibility for the attack, although, needless to say, this was never reported in South Africa.[2]

'The least said the better'

Any media critic would conclude that the Silverton siege represented a clear public relations victory for the police against the pitiable efforts of a cowed and shackled press. Yet just three months later, a study on press coverage of security matters tabled in the South African Parliament urged even tighter constraints on press freedom, while a second 'Steyn Commission' into the Mass Media in 1982 exhorted the South African media to inform the public of the 'total onslaught' to which the country was being subjected by the Soviet Union, the Third World, and even certain circles in the West, concluding that 'government credibility must at all times be maintained and strengthened'. The specific recommendations of these government commissions, ranging from the implementation of a 'National Communication Strategy' to the establishment of a statutory register of journalists from which any could be struck off and banned for life from the profession, raised such a public outcry that the government backed down.

The long-range strategy, it now appears, was not to force such clear abrogations of the cherished ideal of South Africa's 'free press', with all the attendant negative publicity, but rather to win the government bargaining chips for future negotiations with the media.

Anyone doubting the advantage of behind-the-scenes government pressure, as opposed to public regulation of the media, need only glance at a confidential memo issued by the Chief of the South African Defence Force entitled 'Guidelines on Statements in Respect of Incidents of Sabotage and Terrorism: The Need for Security Consciousness and Responsible Reporting'.[3] 'While the need exists for the general public to be informed and reassured concerning acts of terrorism', the memo counsels, 'keeping the public informed must be weighed against providing the enemy with intelligence'. The succinct conclusion: 'As a general rule, "the least said, the better" applies'. The memo goes on to warn spokesmen for the South African Police and Defence Force, victims of attacks, as well as media representatives that, 'in order to deny the enemy intelligence' they should not mention in public statements any of the following information: how the guerrillas entered or left the premises to launch an attack, details of 'enemy casualties (especially if anybody is captured)', or which access routes were followed.

While the professed goal of this memo was 'to deny the enemy the intelligence that would assist him to replan his strategies and methods in an effort to attack the RSA more effectively', this directive also seems geared to operate on an ideological level. As the news management of the Silverton siege so clearly demonstrated, the government feels compelled to suppress the political demands of the ANC because, in the words of Minister of Law and Order Louis le Grange, 'terrorists want publicity for their demands in order to inspire their followers'.

Any outside observer, unencumbered by the fear and ignorance of the ANC so assiduously cultivated by the ruling white minority, would recognize the short-sightedness of such an approach. Banning all reporting of the ANC's strategies and motivations is a transparent attempt at discrediting the organization as a reasonable political movement and portraying its members and leaders as mindless, bloodthirsty anarchists bent on violence purely as a means of instilling terror in the white population and intimidating the black majority. The only sure success of such a policy will be in fanning the fear and ignorance of whites while obscuring any understanding of the grievances of blacks and the real nature of the conflict that is at the root of the current upheavals.

Such a policy seems especially short-sighted in light of the rapid pace of recent events. In late 1985, the editor of the *Cape Times*, one of the very few white members of the commercial press to attempt to push the system of state media control to its limits, risked a three-year prison term by publishing a lengthy interview with ANC President Oliver Tambo. The state's prosecution of Anthony Heard now looks especially pretty in light of the unprecedented decision to allow, and even encourage, the publication of Tambo's New Year's speech less than a month later. Pretoria seems to have concluded — wrongly, in the view of many observers — that the militant tone of the speech would offend more people than it would attract, and the decision was therefore consistent with the government's fixation on reflecting the ANC in the worst possible light. However, the move was certainly inconsistent with Pretoria's long-standing policy of censoring anything to do with the ANC, and thus the overriding impression is one of a leadership thrown totally off balance, unsure of how to manipulate news of its opponents' words and deeds.

Terrorists or freedom fighters

At this juncture it would seem appropriate to pull away, temporarily, from the focus purely on Southern Africa, to note that the tendency to blur any distinction between 'guerrillas', 'freedom fighters' and 'terrorists' is by no mean peculiar to this particular sub-region. North American consumers of the mainstream media are fed a confusing battery of signals for distinguishing the good guys from the bad guys in the reports they get of various conflicts throughout the world. In Central America, for example, the gunmen destabilizing Nicaragua are described by President Reagan as 'the moral equivalent of our founding fathers', while the country's elected government is labelled 'communist' and 'totalitarian'. In Middle Eastern conflicts, the rule of thumb for sniffing out a 'terrorist' masquerading as a 'freedom fighter' lies in his or her relationship with the Palestinian Liberation Organization or, worse yet, links with Libya's Colonel Kadhafi.

With regard to southern Africa outside of South Africa, the criteria become even more obscure. In neighboring Marxist Mozambique, the armed insurgents destabilizing the economy are a recognized scourge that both the US and South Africa claim to want to eradicate. Yet in neighboring Marxist Angola, the seemingly analogous destabilizing force is led by a man embraced by Washington and Pretoria, and described unblushingly by both as a 'freedom fighter'. The height of confusion in this regard was reached recently in Lesotho, where a regime first installed by South Africa found itself deposed with the encouragement, if not direct support, of Pretoria. Black South Africans might well be excused for concluding that the white man's 'terrorist' is the black man's 'freedom fighter' — and vice versa — and that Pretoria and Washington seem to share the same definitions of those terms. Many blacks say that the media's constant reference to the 'Russian-made weapons' and 'Eastern bloc training' used by the ANC's guerilla army may fuel whites' loathing of the Soviet Union and its allies, but it has had the opposite effect on blacks, who see the police and army that oppresses them as Western-supported. As one young Soweto student put it, 'The people regard the West as a friend of their enemy, and you know that the friend of your enemy cannot be your friend'.[4]

The consensus carrot and the press-bashing stick

With laws like the Protection of Information Act, the Internal Security Act, and more than 100 other laws that mock the very concept of 'freedom of the press' in South Africa. The government has almost every conceivable legal means of controlling the flow of news and information to the public. But this is the Republic's self-proclaimed era of reform, and the government is not keen to be seen to be further expanding its legislative arsenal against the media. On the contrary, the credibility of the government's reforms depends on the image of a healthy opposition from within the system — expressed in the context of what the government has called 'consensus journalism'. In mid-1981, on the eve of the first sitting of the tricameral parliament — and the burgeoning mass protests that finally forced President P.W. Botha to declare a State of Emergency a year later — the Minister of Constitutional Development announced that the 'new deal' would require a 'media style' that would highlight 'consensus opportunities' rather than concentrating on 'problems causing conflict'. Minister Chris Heunis went on to explain that, while the government agreed that it was necessary for the media to point out problems, such observations should always be balanced against the 'potential for consensus'.

As it happened, the events of the past eighteen months presented a challenge even to pro-government journalists to emphasize any positive 'potential for consensus', with well over 1,000 blacks killed in township violence, mainly by members of the police and army. As a result, the government suddenly dropped the consensus carrot and once again grabbed the press-bashing stick. Before this latest and most worrying assault on press freedom is detailed, however, an update on the state of the liberal anti-government media is in order.

If there had been one living symbol of the white-run opposition press in South Africa it was Johannesburg's *Rand Daily Mail*, whose editors and reporters were prosecuted for their exposés of prison conditions in the 60s and the Information Scandal (which revealed the existence of illegal propaganda slush funds and cases of government media manipulation) in the 70s. Although the 80s had seen the *Mail*'s image begin to tarnish, especially after the political sacking of its outspoken editor, Allister Sparks, the decision of the Anglo-American Corporation-owned newspaper monopoly to close the paper a year ago still sent shock waves through media circles all over the world. Many observers saw cynical political motives on the part of English capital, which has, in this season of reform, closed ranks with Afrikaner big business and thus no longer needs such a strident anti-government mouthpiece. Other analysts believe that it was, ironically, the *Mail*'s success in championing black causes that ultimately brought it down, for the paper had sought the bulk of its advertising revenues from white business.

Two other English dailies and a black Sunday paper were also closed in the wake of the *Mail*'s demise, and three of the country's five biggest black publications passed from white liberal control to one of the two government-supporting Afrikaans press monpolies. Media critics have begun to worry that 'South Africa's already battered commercial press could end up resembling the Rhodesian press during the last years of Ian Smith's rule, reflecting only the views of a tiny minority'.[5]

The every-narrowing job options for liberal journalists prompted several former editors and reporters to pool their severance pay and launch the independent *Weekly Mail*. Its influence is greater than its few thousand subscribers would indicate, for the paper has become a 'must' to read for foreign journalists and diplomats. If the new *Mail*'s price — more than a rand a copy — puts it out of the reach of most blacks, another new national weekly is aiming to fill that vacuum. Edited by South Africa's top black journalist, Zwelakhe Sisulu (son of Walter Sisulu, an ANC leader imprisoned with Mandela), the *New Nation* is sponsored by the South Africa Catholic Bishops Conference, a group which has demonstrated its courage in taking on government censors by denouncing alleged atrocities committed by security forces in Namibia and the black townships. Both the *Weekly Mail* and the *New Nation* are small and struggling, but the fact that they represent the only significant media voices not controlled by either the government (in the case of the Afrikaans press) or multi-national capital (in the case of the English press) makes them well worth the support of anyone truly committed to the embattled ideal of press freedom.

The TV gag

The most recent installment in the recurring clash between government and the media centers not on the newspapers but rather on the medium of television. South Africa entered the era of 'ungovernability' with enough laws to constrain the words used to describe the mass protests that have engulfed the country, but the pictures emanating from the black townships have been harder to control. The government's first response was to 'blame the messengers' who are bringing the bad tidings of intensifying civil war in South Africa to the rest of the world. During President

Botha's much-derided 'Rubicon' speech of August 1985 (in which he bitterly disappointed even his staunchest Western supporters with a total lack of new initiatives), Botha turned on the electronic media: 'How do they explain the fact that they are always present, with cameras, at places where violence takes place? Are there people from the revolutionary elements who inform them to be ready?' A resident of one of Cape Town's troubled townships wrote to the Johannesburg *Financial Mail* with an apt repartee: 'To continually maintain that sympathetic journalists are acting as catalysts and making actors out of protesters is another example of the unceasing attempts to pass the buck — and the buck stops in Pretoria'.

Sadly enough, for those who aim to bring some conflict resolution to this troubled battleground, the South African government cannot conceive of the notions of fairness and balance in media reporting except in ideological terms. The head of the new state 'Information Bureau', Louis Nel, recently came up with the following game plan for countering overseas TV footage of police violence against township protesters: 'There is little we can do about such impressions apart from inviting cameramen to cover the other side, where, say, police play soccer with township schoolboys, to give a balanced picture'. For Nel, 'the million-dollar question is how to get police to use sjamboks (rawhide whips used in 'riot control') less and soccer more'. Those on the receiving end of the sjambok/soccer media strategy might prefer to see a state response that is geared to their specific grievances and not targeted solely on the National Party's international media image. Furthermore, confidence in the motives behind the Information Bureau is not strengthened by memories of its director's past forays into the field of media relations, for government credibility was sorely strained by the 1985 disclosures of Nel's secret visits to the mountain stronghold of the Mozambican National Resistance army, with which Pretoria was claiming to have cut all ties.

The escalation of the Information Bureau's 'blame-the-messenger' media policy into a more determinedly anti-press freedom policy of 'kill-the-messenger' came with the graphic worldwide television coverage of the State of Emergency. The state-run South African Broadcasting Corporation monopoly was instructed by P.W. Botha as far back as 1980 (seemingly in response to Silverton) 'not to feature reports of the onslaughts on South Africa by revolutionary elements as main news items', thus the footage from the townships that South Africans watch in their living rooms is routinely sanitized. It was not the local TV fare, but rather the tales of what is seen in the living rooms of the rest of the world that began to worry Pretoria in 1985. 'Overseas one is confronted with footage we don't see here at all', reported a white liberal opposition leader after a trip to New York. 'What comes over very clearly is that it's not just a handful of agitators causing unrest in South Africa — it's a whole community in protest'. Similarly, a TV correspondent for a major American network was quoted in an English Sunday paper as saying, 'I know a lot of whites in this country and I don't think any of them has any idea of what is going on a few miles from their homes: the anger, the bitterness and frustration, or the organization and the commitment of the black people'.

It is precisely the spectre of 'a whole community in protest', motivated by 'frustration' and 'commitment' rather than 'a handful of agitators' that the government hopes vainly to excise from public consciousness. The wave of media coverage outside South Africa after the declaration of the State of Emergency was followed, inside South Africa, by a concerted campaign against the foreign media that was disturbing even by South African standards. After a brief, abortive attempt to cajole the media into 'toning down' reporting on the townships, a security force committee was appointed to monitor news coverage, and the battle lines were drawn. A month after the declaration of the State of Emergency, nine media representatives were arrested in Cape Town and charged with obstructing the police in the execution of their duties while covering an attempted march on the prison where the top ANC leadership is being held. The next month, *Newsweek* magazine, which had featured an article on South Africa that was, by all accounts, accurate and fair, had that issue banned from distribution and its correspondent summarily deported. The following month saw journalists barred from entering Soweto. Countless other journalists have had their film and videotapes confiscated and many have even been physically attacked and fired at with teargas, birdshot and rubber bullets by police and soldiers.

Then the smear campaign against the foreign press began, with a suspicious build-up of unbelievable stories, said to emanate from unnamed informants among the foreign press corps and anonymous outraged witnesses, of TV crews allegedly stage-managing phoney unrest scenes by paying black youngsters to riot. (It was later disclosed in the British and South African press that amongst the government's evidence of these alleged media stunts was a letter that proved to be a crude forgery.) The climax of this press-bashing campaign came with an extraordinary Government Gazette in November 1985, banning the use of audio-visual equipment for recording disturbances or unrest situations in the designated emergency areas except with express permission, and then only via police escort.

These restrictions, which effectively keep all TV crews and still photographers well away from 'hot' areas, were immediately denounced by the Johannesburg-based Foreign Correspondents Association as a thinly veiled attempt at a news black-out. The white liberal Progressive Federal Party went so far as to condemn the measure as press 'terrorism' (a term it usually reserves for condemnation of ANC attacks), and charged the government with deluding itself by thinking 'kill the messenger and you've somehow solved the problem, when in fact all you've done is delay the explosion'. The black anti-apartheid activist, Reverend Allan Boesak, went even further. In his first speech since his release from detention (for attempting to organize a peaceful 'Free Mandela' march), Boesak issued this challenge: 'Botha must answer whether the purpose of keeping reporters out of the townships is so that our children can be murdered in circumstances where there will be no witnesses and no record'. Even Britain's Margaret Thatcher, whose exhortations for the world to 'cut the oxygen supply of terrorism' from the media were quoted (out of context) in defense of the media ban, summoned a member of the South African Embassy in London to the Foreign Office to convey official British government displeasure with the latest violation of press freedom.

Psychological warfare

Why, in fact, did Pretoria invite such controversy by invoking the

TV gag? One answer is dictated by 'the bottom line': that South Africa's economy, in the throes of the worst recession in 50 years, could no longer afford to allow the documentation of what appeared to be an inexorable spiral of civil war. In the view of sympathetic foreign analysts, 'With the continued negotiations for foreign loans, the growing disinvestment lobby, and the increasing isolation of Pretoria, it was necessary to get those sjamboks off the screens'.[6] A group of media academics at the University of the Witwatersrand read a more ominous message into the media ban: that it represented a watershed in state repression, signalling a new police and army strategy in the townships 'which would be even more unacceptable to foreign television audiences'.[7] These academics cited an incident in which Cape Town police hidden in boxes on the back of a government transport vehicle drove through a township street and then leapt out, 'like macabre jack-in-the-boxes', when stones were thrown, ambushing unarmed demonstrators (including children) with shotgun fire. The fact that the so-called 'Trojan Horse incident' was filmed and shown on international television is believed to have prompted the media ban. The Witwatersrand academics say that the preconceived nature of such a tactic shows that the authorities have reached the end of an ad hoc response to South Africa's conflict and may be embarking on a more open 'occupation force' strategy which will deploy a combination of military maneuvres and psychological warfare techniques that can only be carried out in a sealed-off 'operational area' over which policemen and soldiers have total control. The academics further noted that the eviction of the media from unrest areas must inevitably add to residents' terror — and compliance, they note, 'can be won by terror as much as by any hearts-and-minds exercise'.

While the government decidedly does not want its terror tactics filmed — hence the media ban — the unabashed propagandists at the South African Broadcasting Corporation seize upon any evidence of brutality from the other side. The government's declaration of the emergency, as broadcast over SABC-TV, was a prime example of how the state can manipulate media imagery toward its own ends. The President's announcement was followed by extensive footage of two incidents filmed in the townships: the mass funeral of four black activists who disappeared and were then found with their bodies grotesquely mutilated, and the 'sell-out killing' of a woman believed to be a police informer. At the Cradock funeral, the head of the South African Council of Churches, Reverend Beyers Naudé, and Reverend Boesak were both filmed so that they appeared to be speaking under the banner of the banned South African Communist Party, although in fact they were on a podium draped with scores of anti-government banners. There was, curiously, no sound as the ministers spoke; the impression left was that they were being inexplicably inflammatory. The SABC then juxtaposed the totally unrelated attack on the Duduza informer, and, at six on a Saturday evening, prime viewing time for young children, the camera lingered on the gruesome spectacle of a young woman being burned to death by a frenzied mob. The TV critic of the *Financial Mail* summed up one widespread response to that piece of agitprop: 'You don't have to be a psychologist to realize that the average viewer will unconsciously perceive a simple causal link: the emergency announcement is justified by the rhetorical behavior of two ministers of religion and the actions of muderers'. The SABC may be banking on most viewers to be taken in by the cheap propaganda trick, but the government may ultimately suffer more from those who will instead be prompted to raise questions, about what those ministers, one white and one black, were saying about the brutal Cradock murders (which were widely held to be the work of the police) and about why the maddened townships got so angry in the first place.

Commercial vs. community media

The government may believe that it has won a battle, now that it has tamed the local press and gagged the foreign media, but in fact it has merely ensured that the war will be that much bloodier, for only an honest understanding of the underlying dynamics of South Africa's conflict can ever bring a resolution. Moreover, the point of departure for one who sincerely wants to reach that understanding should be that all news reports on South Africa must be approached with a critical eye, for every commercial media representative — be he or she South African or foreign, government-supporting or liberal — is subjected to some degree of government control. As a result, the conventional Western notions of media 'objectivity' are grossly distorted, for the leaders and members of mass-based anti-government organizations have to struggle for exposure of their views in the commercial media, while the pronouncements and opinions of the government, government-created 'leaders' such as homeland chiefs and community councillors, and individuals who represent no mass base are all disproportionately represented. Thus, anyone who seeks a representative sample of popular opinion must make a concerted effort to monitor media other than the conventional commercial print and broadcast outlets. One could make a start by buying the 'Extra' or 'Africa' editions of the commercial press (for even the liberal newspapers practice a form of media apartheid and produce different editions aimed at black and white readers) and the various magazines aimed specifically at a black market (although it should be noted that virtually all 'black' publications are published by white-owned concerns).

Reading what the white press prints for blacks at least gives one an idea of what most blacks are reading — though not necessarily endorsing. Blacks in the eastern Cape staged a 10-week boycott of all editions of the East London *Daily Dispatch* after an editorial called Nelson Mandela and other jailed political leaders 'criminals'. Many blacks said the boycott represented a more general dissatisfaction with the paper's political reporting. 'There was a lack of coverage of events in our areas', explained the local publicity secretary of the United Democratic Front, an umbrella group of more than 700 affiliated anti-apartheid organizations. 'And when they did cover anything concerning us it was always one-sided'. When losses to the newspaper's management topped R 40,000 with sales down more than 30 per-cent, the *Dispatch* printed a front-page apology, acknowledging that its editorial policy was seen in some quarters as pro-apartheid.

Unfortunately, blacks and other government opponents cannot usually influence editorial policies through consumer boycotts. Increasing numbers of anti-apartheid activists have given up on the commercial press completely and instead have founded their own community-based newsletters, newspapers and magazines. Like the community organizations which they promote, these publications define local, grassroots fights, in the townships, schools or the workplace, as part of a broader national struggle against apartheid. Community media is rooted in a context — resistance — that is alien to the commercial press. While the commercial press aims to inform and entertain, community media works to raise critical awareness. 'All over South Africa, people are hearing the words of the bosses, and the government TV, the radio, the newspapers and films control what we know and think', wrote Cape Town's *Grassroots* community newspaper recently. 'We need to answer back; we need to speak for ourselves, to find ways of reaching people and passing on our own message. The state uses media to control the people; we must use it to liberate ourselves'. Another key difference between the commercial and the progressive press lies, of course, in the fact that profit is the underlying motive for any commercial paper to publish, while the community media aim only to break even, financially, and often rely more on grant funding than selling advertising.

The rise of community media dates back to 1980, and parallels the mushrooming of the civic associations, student organizations, women's groups, religious bodies and the independent trade union movement, culminating in the launch of the United Democratic Front in 1983 and the Congress of South African Trade Unions in 1985. The state's response to the growing influence of community media has paralleled its reaction to the increasing power of the mass-based organizations: media workers, like community activists are harassed, detained and forced into hiding or exile. The most common form of state repression of community media has been through relentless bannings by the Publications Directorate; one community newspaper even had its offices, along with those of a range of community and union organizations, blown up.

Community media workers have coped, in turn, by expanding their scope. State harassment may handicap the production of an issue of a newspaper, but there are always enough people around to print up some pamphlets, leaflets or handbills. At the height of the State of Emergency, for example, producing the monthly *UDF News* proved impossible, so instead, those leaders not in jail or on the run poured their energy into the printing of several thousand handbills that pleaded to the police, 'Stop Killing us'!

and proclaimed 'Leaders detained, but UDF fights on'. This siege mentality has spurred the development and sophistication of new media forms: Johannesburg's Silkscreen Training Project finds itself fighting a constant battle against time, in an effort to get its posters and T-shirts out to meetings (and lately, funerals) before the censorship authorities declare them 'banned for distribution'. The quest for unbannable media has led to a pro-liferation of freedom songs, bumper stickers, political graffiti, and, the latest innovation, the placing of placard-bearing dummies on lampposts and park benches, where they are seen by hundreds of passers-by before they are confiscated by police. Each new political development brings its media counterpart, as the very definition of community media expands daily. Boycotting students hold alternative education workshops. Protesting town-ship residents stage candle-lit vigils, and when the police baton-charge them in the streets, the people retreat into their homes and second a message via a single candle in the front window of every family's home.

In conclusion, then, anyone interested in the resolution of the conflict in Southern Africa must take up the challenge of becoming not just a conscientious media consumer, but a media critic and researcher as well. Ideally, one should be exposed to a range of media, from government hand-outs to the 'Radio Freedom' program broadcast by the African National Congress. It is worth bearing in mind that the publications once banned by the white minority government of Rhodesia, such as the Catholic magazine, *Moto*, and the Zimbabwe African National Union's monthly, *Zimbabwe News*, are now sold on the streets of Harare alongside *Time* and the *Financial Gazette*. Just as today's political prisoner could become tomorrow's Prime Minister, it is not unthinkable that today's community newspapers could be training the journalists who will one day play a central editorial role in the media of a future, non-racial South Africa.

Note on the author: Julie Frederikse is the author of *South Africa: A Different Kind of War*, (forthcoming from James Currey, U.K.) and *None But Ourselves: Masses vs. Media in the Making of Zimbabwe* (Penguin, U.S., 1984 and Heinemann, U.K., 1983). She has served as Southern Africa correspondent

96

for National Public Radio (U.S.) since 1979, based first in Johannesburg and now in Harare, and also reports for *Africa-Asia* magazine, the Canadian Broadcasting Corporation and the BBC.

Notes

1. 'Craig Tyson's Eyewitness Report: Confusion and Blood' *Bulletin*, Rhodes University Journalism Department, Vol. 2, No. 1, 1980.
2. Stephen Davis, *Season of War: Insurgency in South Africa*, forthcoming from Yale University Press.
3. Julie Frederikse, *South Africa: A Different Kind of War*, James Currey, UK, (June) 1986.
4. *Ibid*.
5. 'Behind Closed Doors: Media Murders', *Work in Progress*, No. 36, 1985. See also Julie Frederikse, *None But Ourselves: Masses vs. Media in the Making of Zimbabwe*, Viking-Penguin, US, 1984; Heinemann, UK, 1983; Zimbabwe Publishing House, 1983; Ravan Press, Johannesburg, 1982.
6. Harriet Gavshon, Eric Louw and Ray Williams, 'Shut Your Eyes and Think of Nothing', *Weekly Mail*, November 8—14, 1986.
7. *Ibid*.

THE CORPORATE INVESTOR AND THE PROCESS OF CHANGE IN SOUTH AFRICA

Millard W. Arnold
President, Associates International

It is now almost universally accepted that the decline and fall of apartheid is inevitable in South Africa. At issue is whether the end will come as a result of evolutionary change, violent confrontation, or protracted negotiations. Barring the sudden, and totally unexpected collapse of the Pretoria Government, it will presumably take a substantial period of time to bring about the demise of apartheid through either change, violence or negotiation. Because evolutionary change is a gradual process in which only agonizing slowness can bring meaningful results, violence is likely to be closely associated with any such attempt. Indeed, evolutionary change is itself, more often than not, a response to violent confrontation. It tends to pit those seeking to preserve as much of a status quo as possible, against those willing to implement a more responsive, even radical alternative. Such is the case in South Africa today. Faltering efforts at reform are met by massive displays of violence as the struggle for a more just society continues. Moreover, because the conflict has spilled over into the neighboring countries, it has had a profoundly debilitating impact on the possibility of peace and security for the entire Southern Africa region. Given that the forces of change and violence are so finely balanced in South Africa, neither side is likely to prevail over the other, suggesting that some measure of negotiation will ultimately prove the only lasting solution.

As South Africa tilts precariously on the edge of revolution, those who see negotiation as the most desirable alternative have attempted to formulate approaches and involve institutions that can ensure a meaningful transition with a minimum of violence.

As that effort unfolds, increasingly, the corporate investor has become a focus of attention. Indeed, few subjects have proven as controversial as the issue of whether or not foreign corporate investment can play a significant role in the process of political and social change in South Africa. Many argue that those companies that invest in South Africa are directly or indirectly responsible for maintaining apartheid, the ideology of racial discrimination, and that by complying with the country's legal and social institutions, they cannot help but reinforce its practice. In response, it has been argued that the continued corporate presence in South Africa is beneficial to the black population of the country and that business activities contribute to the erosion of apartheid. Indeed, it is widely accepted by many both within and outside South Africa that the business community represents the most potent of all forces for change.[1]

Over the past two and a half years, South Africa has been engulfed in a massive wave of civil unrest which, in July of last year, forced the country's President, P.W. Botha, to declare a state of national emergency. The fury of black South Africans, the extent and nature of the violence, and the increasing use of work stoppages and consumer boycotts, led to a dramatic loss of confidence in the Botha government. Alarmed by the unrest, South Africa's financial creditors refused to renew short term credit, which exacerbated the country's political difficulties and plunged South Africa into an immediate and devastating economic crisis.

Yet, the violent upheaval of the black community should have come as no surprise to government and business leaders. Black frustration had been well documented in an August 1984 survey conducted by Lawrence Schlemmer, a sociologist at the University of Natal. Professor Schlemmer had been commissioned by the US State Department to explore the attitudes and industrial issues among blacks in South Africa. His study, 'Black Worker Attitudes: Political Options, Capitalism and Investment in South Africa', was intended to show the support of blacks for foreign invesment. It was far more revealing about the current mood of black South Africans. According to the study:

(a) between 65—70 percent of black South Africans were either unhappy, or impatient or angry about the quality of their life;

(b) 84 percent saw the situation staying the same or getting worse and;

(c) 61 percent were willing to take political risk in order to bring about change.[2]

Professor Schlemmer's study graphically pointed out that nearly two-thirds of the black population was seething, awaiting some form of political explosion, and, more importantly, most were willing to take the chance to bring such an explosion about. While the immediate focus of black anger was social and economic, at the core of black discontentment was the denial of political rights and representation.

As South Africa's black population escalate their demands for social and political justice, and as general conditions within the country continue to deteriorate, the demand for the imposition of sanctions and the withdrawal of corporate investments from South Africa is increasingly being made throughout Europe and the United States.

The movement for divestment is fueled by the realization that approximately 10 percent of the country's total investment or between $15.5 and $17 billion comes from foreign corporate investors.[3] According to a report issued by the United Nations Commission on Transnational Corporations, investors from two countries, Britain and the United States, are responsible for nearly 70 percent of all the investment in South Africa.[4] West Germany with 10 percent, France with between 5 and 10 percent, Switzerland with between 5 and 10 percent and Canada with approximately 1 percent are the other major corporate investors.[5] Foreign direct investment is substantial in sectors such as petroleum, motor vehicles, chemicals, electronics and banking. While direct foreign investment constitutes 10 percent of South Africa's total investment, an additional 20 percent of capital stock is held by foreigners in portfolio investment.[6]

British companies are by far the largest single corporate investors with more than $8 billion or half of the direct foreign investment in South Africa.[7] For Britain, the stakes in South Africa are enormous. Approximately $14 billion is directly or indirectly invested in South Africa, representing 10 percent of total British foreign investment.[8] According to the International Monetary Fund's 1985 Direction of Trade Statistics, in 1984, South Africa exported $742 million to Britain and imported $1.66 billion.[9] The number of British jobs directly dependent on South African trade is about 150,000.[10]

The United States has between 18 and 20 percent of total direct investment in South Africa.[11] US direct investment in South Africa has gone from $490 million in 1966 to a peak of $2.6 billion in 1981.[12] The U.S. State Department calculated a direct investment figure for 1983 of $2.3 billion and $7 billion in portfolios, for a total direct and indirect investment of $9.3 billion.[13] The United States is South Africa's largest trading partner. In 1984, South African exports to the United States were worth $1.45 billion and imports from the United States totaled $2.37 billion.[14]

With so much at stake, corporate investors are not simply the targets of the divestment movement — they conceivably have the leverage to profoundly influence the social and political issues that affect black and white South Africa. But the question remains, given the nature of business, it is the responsibility of the corporate sector to address moral questions and seek to transform an unjust society? Or should the responsible corporate role be to allow political issues to be resolved through the political process including the possibility of massive civil unrest? In view of the political realities that characterize South Africa today, is it possible for South Africa's corporate community — both domestic and foreign — to be a major factor in the process of change? In short, what can, and should be realistically expected from the corporate investor?

The smoldering black townships, a more militant black trade union movement, the increasing use of black consumer boycotts, and an economy in crisis, were certainly all good reasons for business to pressure government about the necessity of political reform. Moreover, international support for economic sanctions against South Africa and the growth of the divestment movement in the United States put increasing pressure on the corporate investors to justify their presence in the country by becoming more actively involved in the process of change.

In March 1985, following 18 months of continuous civil unrest, the American Chamber of Commerce in South Africa submitted a memorandum to the South African government on a broad range of issues aimed at fostering economic integration and peaceful change in the country. On the crucial issue of democratic participation, it noted that:

> '. . . an appropriate political formula for South Africa can only be arrived at by South Africans themselves through an agreed process of negotiation in which representatives of all race groups and political parties can freely participate. For such a process of negotiation to be effective, it must necessarily include leaders or organizations now proscribed and/or operating in exile.[15]

In the context of South Africa, the position taken by the American Chamber of Commerce was nothing short of extra-ordinary. For the first time, a business organization was publicly calling for serious, in depth negotiations between black and white as a means of determining the country's political future. More importantly, it was suggesting that a precondition for viable negotiations, the government would have to release Nelson Mandela and other incarcerated opposition leaders, and that any talks on the country's future would have to include the banned African National Congress.[16]

In August, following the declaration of a state of emergency in large parts of the country, the two major English-speaking business associations, the Federated Chamber of Industries and the Associated Chambers of Commerce joined the Urban Foundation and the National African Chamber of Commerce, to issue a press statement that expressed the same need for a nego-tiated settlement with 'accepted leaders of the black community even if some of these are currently in detention'.[17] While the Afrikaanse Handelsinstituut, the Afrikaner business association, was unwilling to endorse any statement that suggested negotiating with Mandela or the ANC, in January of 1985 it had joined with five other employer organizations representing 'more than 80 percent of the employment strength of the country', to issue a public statement committing themselves to furthering 'an ongoing process of economic and political reform in the Republic'.[18]

The willingness of South African businessmen and foreign corporate investors to address what had previously been considered 'political' issues, is a fairly recent phenomena motivated in great part by enlighted self-interest, and in part by a level of hysteria and fear that is always close to the surface during periods of turmoil in South Africa. The current spate of activity comes at a time when by all accounts, the rage and anger of the black community has never been greater. Thousands of lives have been lost, and the government has all but conceded that it can only control the black townships through massive use of force.

Yet, the intentions of South African businessmen and foreign corporate investors in purporting to call for social change are increasingly questioned by the black community on whose behalf such efforts are undertaken. Of concern to the black community is the seemingly irreconcilable difference between business on the one hand, and blacks on the other as to what is precisely meant by change. For business, change means the beginning of negotiations toward the establishment of a stable political climate in which blacks and whites share power. It is a position that affords the maximum benefits to business. The extent of powersharing, the structure of the expanded political system and the speed with which the political reforms should be carried out are but issues to be resolved.

For most blacks, however, change can only mean but one thing, and that is negotiations that lead to a fundamental transfer of power — the realization of the democratic ideal of 'one person, one vote in a unitary state'. For blacks, that democratic principle is a non-negotiable agenda item. Yet, by and large, South African businessmen have consistently rejected the notion of one person, one vote in a unitary state, arguing as Gavin Relly of the Anglo American Corporation did in the *New York Times*,

'I'm not in favor of one man, one vote in South Africa. It would be simply a formula for unadulterated chaos at this point in time in our history'.[19]

The chasm that currently separates the interest of the corporate sector from the aspirations of the black community reveals the level of distrust that generally exists when blacks are questioned regarding their views of business. As the Schlemmer study points out, 100 percent of U.S. company employees and 91 percent of most blacks felt that business worked with and supported the government, while 73 percent thought that business did not help blacks by appealing to government.[20]

Given the divergent positions held by business and the black community, it is increasingly obvious that in the context of South Africa today, change means either gradual social and economic reform designed to maintain control, or a fundamental transfer of power. Clearly, then, the role of the corporate investor is determined by how change is defined. If change means gradual reform, then the role of the corporate investor is limited. What corporations currently do in South Africa, while hardly adequate, may suffice. If, however, change means a transfer of power, then in essence the corporation must support black demands for a restructured society. That in turn confronts the corporation with two conflicting and painful choices: disinvest or seek the establishment of a new social order that may be inimical to its own interests.

Although certain segments of the business community have called for the release of Nelson Mandela, and initiated contacts with the exiled African National Congress in Lusaka, Zambia, they have been drawn primarily from the English-speaking business elite, which has had but a marginal impact on the thinking of the largely Afrikaner government.

While black South Africans are less than optimistic about business being an agent for change, paradoxically, that view is seemingly shared to some degree by the Botha government as well. Although Pretoria recognizes the importance of business in generating economic growth, it thus far has been unwilling to heed the corporate call for negotiations. The government's reticence is explained by the realization that the issues that would be the subject of negotiation would fundamentally undermine the ability of whites to maintain power.

Aware that change is necessary, but committed to the continuation of white rule in some acceptable form, the Botha government has sought means of introducing peripheral reforms while tightly controlling the process of any meaningful change.

In the highly polarized environment of South Africa, the distrust that blacks have toward the motives and intentions of the corporate community, and the trauma that government experiences when it considers the prospects of change, suggest that there is very little that the corporate investor can do to facilitate any substantial transformation of South African society.

To some degree, by calling for negotiations, pressing for the release of Mandela, recognizing the ANC and pushing government to appreciate the urgency of the current situation, business has already served a useful purpose. Unless it intends to fully exercise its economic clout by refusing to pay taxes or disinvesting, business will largely become irrelevant in the course of events that are playing themselves out in South Africa. With black unemployment reaching 50 percent in several urban areas and thousands of children boycotting schools, there exist the volatile, combustive ingredients that are certain to lead to further violence, further unrest. As the turmoil, and resulting economic chaos takes its toll, the government will ultimately be forced to negotiate as white resolve collapses in the face of sustained, unrelenting pressure from the black community.

As conditions inside the country become untenable, the corporate investors will, individually, elect to take steps to reduce their exposure. Ironically, such action may be the most significant role that the business community can take to insure the possibility of peaceful change. Indeed, if any single event serves to galvanize the South African government to reserve its position on releasing Mandela and negotiating with the ANC, it will prove to have been the decision in August 1985, by Chase Manhattan Bank, Citibank, and other US banks, not to extend South Africa's $9 billion in short-term credits. That decision, taken by the major financial institutions in the United States, reflected a purely business judgment that further investment in South Africa would be a substantially bad risk. Other banks soon followed, thereby reducing South Africa's ability to obtain additional credits, hampering trade and limiting the likelihood of any new foreign investment.

Pretoria responded by suspending payments on its foreign debt in an effort to negotiate a repayment schedule. However, a major obstacle was the insistence by the financial community that South Africa undertake meaningful steps towards social and political reform. Implicit was the need for South Africa to being a process of negotiation that would reduce the political tensions within the country. In January, Botha responded with a major address which, among other things, called for the establishment of a black advisory council in the recently expanded South African Parliament. More importantly, rumors persist that Mandela will be released shortly following 23 years of imprisonment. Should that occur, the pressure of the international banking community will have played no small part.

However, the release of Mandela will not, in and of itself, immediately secure peace or change in South Africa. If Mandela is released, the government's intent will be to begrudgingly meet the conditions established by the international financial community as being necessary for a rescheduling of South Africa's credit. With a revived economy, the hope is that South Africa will be able to create new jobs that will eliminate some of the black unemployment while at the same time provide the country with the resources necessary to finance limited reform. In all likelihood, the violence will not abate and greater pressure for sanctions or divestment will accelerate.

If South Africa is to avoid a prolonged period of mounting urban unrest, some combination of sanctions and selective divestment will be required. To be most effective, sanctions and divestment activities should be directed at those companies that supply critically needed products to the South African police and military. In addition, those companies which furnish technology and strategic goods such as refined petroleum products, communications equipment and computers should have sanctions applied against them. Efforts in this direction have already begun in the United States with the boycott of Shell Oil Company. Moreover, sanctions should be applied against those companies involved in developing projects of strategic importance which enhances the government's ability to maintain the political dominance of whites over the majority black population.[21]

As a means of bringing about change, FOSATU, the Federation of South African Trade Unions, and CUSA, the Council of Unions of South Africa, both adopted resolutions expressing support for divestment although not the withdrawal of companies presently in South Africa. FOSATU and NUM, the National Union of Mineworkers, have merged to create COSATU, the Congress of South African Trade Unions, a highly politicized federation with half a million members that has put political goals at the top of its agenda. Furthermore, in 1985, the United States, Japan, France and Canada all imposed partial restrictions on their economic relations with South Africa.[22] In addition, the British Commonwealth has threatened to impose sanctions in April if there is no indication of political change. While there is little doubt that sanctions would involve some sacrifice for the black community, the longer-term benefits of a possible political solution as a result of the application of sanctions, far outweigh the short-term costs.

Although sanctions and withdrawals will certainly have a negative impact on the South African economy, they will not be enough to cause it to collapse. That, to some degree, is important because while a transfer of power is critical to internal peace and security, a strong, vibrant, majority-ruled South Africa would also contribute to economic growth throughout the region and for the continent as a whole. South Africa, and the Southern Africa region represents Africa's best hope for the future if the continent is to overcome the economic plague that seems so pervasive.

For that scenario to be realized, economic growth will increasingly depend on the private sector. The greatest concentration of corporate strength on the continent of Africa is in South Africa. There is little question that the business community has a significant role to play, both domestically and regionally, once an equitable solution has been reached in South Africa. The issue is, however, what should be the proper function of business in the transitional period between white and black rule? What can business do that will reduce the violence and expedite a transfer of power? While neither the government or the black community seem particularly enamored with the efforts of the corporate sector to engender a climate suitable for negotiations, it must be noted, and indeed stressed, that business has nonetheless taken the all important first step from which other steps may follow.

More importantly, while the corporate community may have a limited role as an agent for change, it is possible for investors to contribute greatly as agents for negotiation. The distinction being that, while the cannot bring about change, they can conceivably facilitate change. As an agent for negotiation, the corporate community's purpose would be simply to bring both sides together. It is a function that investors are particularly well suited to handle, having gained enormous experience in negotiating with labor unions, governments or other corporate entities. As mediators, what could corporations do?

(a) spell out the conditions they fell necessary for meaningful change;
(b) seek to clarify bargaining positions of both sides;
(c) convene a process that begins what is known in diplomatic circles as 'proximity talks';
(d) negotiate with trade unions a joint management-labor position on change; and
(e) explore the possibility of relocating operations to neighboring states;

While all of these are measures that may help the negotiation process, in reality, the likelihood that the business community can continue to serve as a bridge between the majority black population and the South African government is dependent on factors far beyond its control. As one commentator has poignantly noted:

'To date, the protests of black South Africans have awakened businessmen to the need for a reform agenda that is more political and less workplace oriented and have encouraged them to work harder for its acceptance by Pretoria. But this could change if the South African government's continued foot-dragging on reform and its repressive responses to black opposition result in an escalation of violence that spills over into the white community. In that case, business calls for reform could very well become a casualty of a new spiral of violence in South Africa'.[23]

108

Notes

1. 'US investment in South Africa — the $2.5 billion question', Advertisement supplement furnished by the South African Department of Information.
2. Lawrence Schlemmer's 1984 Report, 'Black Worker Attitudes: Political Options, Capitalism and Investment in South Africa' is available from the Centre of Applied Social Sciences, University of Natal, Durban, South Africa. See also September 1985 survey conducted by Mark Orkin of the Community Agency for Social Enquiry (Johannesburg), in association with the Institute for Black Research (Durban).
3. 'Examination of the Activities of Transnational Corporations in South Africa and Namibia', UN Commission on Transnational Corporations, Doc. E/C. 10/AC.4/1985/3, p. 4—5, August 8, 1985.
4. 'Examination of the Activities of Transnational Corporations in South Africa and Namibia', p. 15—18.
5. *Ibid*.
6. *Ibid*.
7. *Ibid*.
8. *The Washington Post*, 7 August 1985.
9. *Financial Mail* Survey on Britain, 16 November 1984.
10. John de St. Jorre, 'South Africa's Non-US Economic Links', CSIS Africa Notes, No. 43, May 24, 1985.
11. *The Washington Post*, 7 August 1985.
12. *Ibid*.
13. *Ibid*.
14. *Ibid*.
15. See Appendix A.
16. For an excellent discussion on the potential role of business in affecting change in South Africa, see generally, David Hauck, *Can Pretoria Be Moved? the emergence of business activism in South Africa*, Investor Responsibility Research Center Inc., 1986.
17. See Appendix C.
18. See Appendix B.
19. Quoted in Hauck's, *Can Pretoria Be Moved?*, p. 36.
20. The Schlemmer Report. See also Orkin survey.

21. Hauck, unpublished manuscript.
22. Hauck, p. 7.
23. Hauck, p. 45.

Appendix A

Summary of proposals submitted to the South African government on March 7, 1985, by the American Chamber of Commerce in South Africa

On March 7, the American Chamber of Commerce in South Africa submitted a series of recommendations to the Special Cabinet Committee under the chairmanship of the Minister of Constitutional Development and Planning. The following is Amcham's summary of its proposals:

The proposals specifically call for all political parties and racial groups in South Africa to begin to work out among themselves an end to racial discrimination. The following steps, if taken, would foster economic integration and peaceful change in the country — and carry forward the process of political and social reform.

Influx control. The proposals call for an end to restrictions on the right of workers to move freely within the country. Indeed, the process of urbanization cannot be arrested indefinitely and urbanization is a prerequisite for broad economic growth.

Housing. Freehold property rights should be granted to all urban blacks in recognition of the permanence of black South African townships.

Removals. The practice of 'removing' blacks, coloreds and Indians from communities closed to them by the Group Areas Act should be phased out. These transfers, often carried out by coercion, result in deprivation and stress for those affected by this policy.

Migrant labor. A migratory labor system that frequently separates spouses and families should be dismantled. After doing so, the government could call upon the private sector to assist it in developing additional housing and infrastructure resources.

Business rights. The opening of the country's major business districts to businessmen of all races is essential to the free enterprise system and to a desegregated society.

Local government. Steps should be taken to fund services in black townships located in white areas. However, the existence of local black authorities is not a substitute for the parliamentary franchise.

Regional government. Cooperative regional government offers a golden opportunity for an experiment in consultation and negotiation between blacks and other groups. The proposals urge the eight economic development regions to include blacks in the decision-making process.

Citizenship and extension of the franchise. Black South Africans should not be denied citizenship on the grounds that they are already citizens of various tribal homelands. This reasoning is contrary to international law and the political will of the majority of the black population. The proposals urge the government to announce its intention to grant the parliamentary franchise to blacks according to a formula to be agreed upon by the leaders of all population groups.

Negotiations for democratic participation. Government should rest upon the consent of the governed. No matter what form a constitutional settlement takes, the future government of South Africa should evolve out of negotiations among representatives of all the races and political parties. These negotiations should begin as soon as possible, and include members of organizations now proscribed or operating in exile.

Appendix B

Press statement by the Die Afrikaanse Handelsinstituut
Association of Chambers of Commerce of South Africa,
Chamber of Mines of South Africa, National African Federation of
Chambers of Commerce, Federated Chamber of Industries, and
Steel and Engineering Industries Federation of South Africa on
March 14, 1985, pledging support for reform in South Africa

1. On 7 January 1985 six South African employer bodies, representing more than 80 percent of the employment strength of
   of country, issued a public statement commiting themselves
   to furthering 'an ongoing process of economic and political
   reform in the Republic'. Critical issues explicitly mentioned
   were:

   — full participation by all South Africans in a private enterprise
     economy and in the political dispensation of the country.
   — a common loyalty to the country as expressed through
     citizenship for all South Africans.
   — ending the forced removal of people.
   — the administration of justice to be safeguarded by the courts.
   — the further development of a free and independent trade
     union movement.

2. Realism dictates that economic and political reforms in South
   Africa must be pursued on their own merits. Nevertheless, the

organizations are keenly aware of the positive impact which visible progress along this road is likely to have an overseas opinion and especially on the current disinvestment debate in the United States.

3. Since the January declaration by organized business in South Africa a number of important statements of intent have been officially announced by the State President and other Cabinet Ministers. These include:

— freehold title to property for blacks.
— resolving the issue of citizenship.
— the suspension of forced removals of people.
— de-emphasizing negative influx control measures in favor of a positive urbanization strategy.
— reaffirmation of the government's commitment to attaining equal education and training opportunities for all South Africans.
— the probable scrapping of racially based marriage and sex laws.
— racially mixed business trading areas.
— the creation of a forum to negotiate black constitutional development up to the highest level based on the explicit recognition of the permanence of blacks in urban areas.
— increased involvement of black in statutory and other decision-making bodies.

4. The signatory organizations welcome and fully endorse these significant statements of intent. Nevertheless, it is vitally important that visible expression is given to these intentions. Accordingly a meeting was arranged with the Minister of Cooperation and Development and Education, Minister Gerrit Viljoen, who has the responsibility for the practical implementation of most of the reforms announced. The organizations offered their full cooperation and assistance in generating concrete results as soon as possible. Each organization will make its contribution according to the expertise and resources at its disposal, on an issue by issue basis. This offer was accepted and the necessary channels of communication explored to facilitate effective cooperation with the various Ministers concerned.

5. The initiatives outlined above have the full support of the American Chamber of Commerce in South Africa and the broad spectrum of American companies in South Africa.

6. The organizations are confident that the full participation of the business community in implementing the important reforms which have been announced will underpin stability and economic development in South Africa and thus accelerate the process of peaceful change which is already under way. In addition, organized business will urge further reforms in terms of their January public declaration. These actions should, in particular, make a considerable ongoing contribution towards realizing the legitimate economic and political aspirations of black South Africans.

Appendix C

Joint statement by the Association of Chambers of Commerce (ASSOCOM), South African Federated Chamber of Industries (FCI), National African Federated Chamber of Commerce and Industries (NAFCOC), and Urban Foundation, on August 29, 1985, in response to the temporary suspension of trading on foreign exchange markets in South Africa and on the Johannesburg stock exchange.

1. The above organizations, representing the great majority of commerce and industry in South Africa, both black and white, are deeply concerned about the deteriorating state of the economy, culminating in the temporary closure of the stock exchange and the foreign exchange market. While there is little doubt that at present economic fundamentals are sound, it is clearly necessary to overcome the prevailing negative political perceptions through positive and imaginative action to restore business confidence. Businessmen all over the country stand ready to develop South Africa aggressively, to seek out new investment opportunities and to create much needed employment. It is, however, impossible to do this in the current climate of political instability.

2. The organizations reaffirm their strong support for a process of peaceful accommodation of the political, social and economic aspirations of all South Africans regardless of race, color or creed. Recently, some important shifts in the dynamics of this

process have occurred which give rise to new opportunities as well as risks both for government and business.

3. There can be no doubt that considerable progress has already been made in many areas to improve the quality of life especially of urban blacks. Further important steps have recently been announced opening the way for rapid progress on employment creation through privatisation, deregulation and the further development of small businesses, whether formal or informal.

4. Nevertheless, the country is at present under considerable pressure. Much of it is related directly or indirectly to the current violence and unrest in black townships. Underlying this situation is a deep mainstream of legitimate black aspirations seeking recognition and accommodation in decision-making structures up to the highest level. This is a major dynamic of South African Society which security action alone cannot resolve. Such aspirations will have to be addressed by a process of serious negotiation with the whole spectrum of accepted black leaders.

5. Government has indeed very recently restated its fundamental commitment to securing a new constitutional dispensation through negotiation. It deserves full support for this commitment. Nevertheless, the process of negotiation itself is still being inhibited by black concern both over the sincerity of government's intentions and the integrity of the bargaining structures which government has set up.

6. No real negotiation is possible without normalizing the security situation through lifting the partial state of emergency as soon as circumstances permit. Equally essential is a commitment by government that it will deal even-handedly with the accepted leaders of the black community, even if some of these are currently in detention.

7. In the area of negotiation with blacks, commerce and industry have in recent years been in the front line. Implementing the new labor dispensation (to accommodate legalized black trade unions) has brought fresh insights and much experience. That background suggests that the following approach could contribute towards breaking the current stalement.

(a) Prior to formal negotiation, the agenda to be discussed must be determined. Unless all relevant black and white leaders can be assured during this pre-negotiation stage that the issues which they regard as vital to their own respective futures will indeed be subject to serious negotiation, they are unlikely to come to the bargaining table.

(b) In turn, an effective dialogue aimed at agenda setting can occur only if government states publicly a clear acceptance of an open-ended agenda.

(c) Once the essential agenda points have been cleared with all accepted black and white leaders, the negotiation process can begin. Certain basic assurances or pre-conditions from government may well be necessary, such as, for example, an undertaking to move away from racial discrimination in the affairs of state. But these will also emerge during the agenda-setting phase.

8. Against the background of their substantial bargaining experience the organizations pledge their full support for such a program of action. They are wholly prepared to utilize, either individually or collectively, what credibility they have with the various parties involved to facilitate a process of mediation and bargaining about the essential agenda to serve as the basis for subsequent negotiation about reform. It is their perception that in so doing they have a crically important but essentially temporary window of opportunity through which they can assist the dynamics of change in South Africa.

9. It is in this spirit of mediation that Nafcoc recently requested government for permission to visit Mr. Nelson Mandela to discuss with him the realities and risks of the process of constitutional reform in South Africa. In addition Nafcoc wishes to assist in clearing the way for his own release, as well as that of other political detainees, albeit on an unconditional basis.

10. The organizations are convinced that in the interests of getting evenhanded and credible negotiations with all accepted black leaders off the ground, a formula must be found to allow these leaders to participate in the essential agenda-setting process outlined above.

11. The politics of negotiation apart, the organizations have serious misgivings about a possible negative economic policy reaction by the domestic authorities to the pressures which currently abound. Organized business would seriously warn against the danger of the country entering a state of siege in response to the threat of local boycotts, trade union strikes and stayaways, and international sanctions and disinvestment.

12. Extended use of direct controls and rationing devices in the areas of foreign exchange, imports, prices and wages, will fundamentally reverse the current trend away from bureaucratic intervention in private business decision-making. In addition, the loss of direct access to international markets, finance and technological transfer will lead inexorably to a decline in international competitiveness. In these crucial areas, unlike Rhodesia in the UDI years, South Africa will stand much more alone.

13. As a reaction to political pressures, a siege economy essentially treat symptoms rather than causes. The panoply of discretionary government controls which it implies will lead over time to

   — lower standards of living for all South Africans
   — depressed average rates of growth
   — a poor investment climate leading to little new domestic investment coupled with limited entry of new entrepreneurs into the economy, especially of small businesses, whether black or white
   — a high rate of unemployment
   — strong inflationary pressures

14. Of major concern to investors, both foreign and domestic, is political stability coupled with reasonable after-tax returns. The critical problems facing South Africa in these areas cannot be resolved by retreating into economic isolationism and a controlled economy. Our survival depends on making the necessary structural changes to uphold the political, social and economic values pursued by our major trading partners which represent, in essence, the great democracies of the world. Should we fail to do so, investors and traders will increasingly

shy away from South Africa, without any formal laws forcing them to do so.

15. For their part, the organizations will remain actively involved in a broad-ranging program of project orientated research and mediation among all interest groups on critical issues facing the country, including

— exploring and discussing various constitutional options for South Africa
— a positive urbanization policy aimed inter alia at substantial employment creation and abolishing influx control and the pass laws
— developing equitable and effective policy guidelines for privatisation, deregulation and the active development of small business enterprises, both formal and informal
— eliminating obstacles in the way of securing a common citizenship for all South Africans
— introducing at central policy level a non-discriminatory and vocation orientated education policy which will intra alia open opportunities for black advancement and remove the constraints on productivity and competitiveness in the country.

16. In conclusion, the organizations wish to emphasize that normalizing the South African situation can only come about if all the country's people recognize that they have a shared destiny to be arrived at through serious negotiation between partners of equal negotiating status. The organizations again dedicate themselves towards achieving this fundamental goal and in so doing restore confidence and credibility in South Africa.

Appendix D

Advertisement by US and South African businessmen in the
Johannesburg Sunday Times on September 29, 1985
'There is a better way'

As responsible businessmen committed to South Africa and the welfare of all its people, we are deeply concerned about the current situation.

We believe that the reform process should be accelerated by:

(a) Abolishing statutory race discrimination wherever it exists;
(b) Negotiating with acknowledged black leaders about power sharing;
(c) Granting full South African citizenship to all our peoples;
(d) Restoring and entrenching the rule of law.

We reject violence as a means of achieving change and we support the politics of negotiation.

We believe that there is a better way for South Africa and we support equal opportunity, respect for the individual, freedom of enterprise and freedom of movement.

We believe in the development of the South African economy for the benefit of all of its people and we are, therefore, committed to pursue a role of corporate social responsibility and to play our part in transforming the structures and systems of the country toward fair participation for all.

INSIDE SOUTH AFRICA – THE PLAYERS AND THEIR ROLE IN SOCIAL CHANGE: THE LABOR UNIONS

Penelope Andrews
La Trobe University

'With the acceptance of the Wiehahn report there will in future be no distinction between blacks and whites; gradually more blacks will be introduced to fill the traditional jobs at present held by whites. . . the government committed the greatest treachery against the white employees of South Africa since 1922. . . .'

Mr. Arrie Paulus, General Secretary, Mine Workers Union (white)

'The publicity afforded to this report can only be seen. . . as shocking and provocative. Fortunately it is not yet legislation, and we can only hope that the Minister and the government in their wisdom will exercise good discretion and fulfill their responsibility toward the workers *who have built this country*. . .' (Emphasis added)

Mr. Wessel Bornman, General Secretary, South African Iron, Steel and Allied Industries Union (white)

'Now that we've had the benefit of ministerial interpretation of the Wiehahn Commission some of the fears of the African workers and those unions committed to non-racial unionism are rapidly being confirmed. . . .'

Mr. Alec Erwin, [then] General Secretary, Federation of South African Trade Unions.

The juxtaposition of the attitude of white registered trade

unions with that of the black and non-racial independent, largely unregistered trade union movement reveals the diverse viewpoints and interests between black and white workers within the South African industrial system.[1] As a 'labor aristocracy',[2] white workers have always been sheltered under the umbrella of the Industrial Conciliation Act 28 of 1956, specifically through the Job Reservation clause in that statute.[3]

A lengthy account of the origins of the racist hierarchical division of labor within the working classes in present day South Africa is not within the scope of this paper. It is sufficient for our purposes to note that a social division of labor developed after the discovery of gold and diamonds in South Africa (roughly from 1860 onwards), in which the most senior positions (intellectual, supervisory and skilled manual work) were reserved for whites. Moreover, preferential access to these senior positions was allocated to white through various mechanisms, most specifically unequal education. The South African government also pursued a decisive policy of enshrining racism into every aspect of the formal, registered trade union structure. The Industrial Conciliation Act of 1956 also denied registered status to 'mixed' unions by requiring separate racial or parallel unions for 'colored' and Indian members.

The formation and reproduction of such a division of labor coincided with the requirements of capitalist production in agriculture, manufacturing and mining, and with the political interests of the ruling strata. The resultant inequality is manifest in the fact that the 72% African population takes home 29% of the country's wages, while the white 16% of the population takes home 59% of the national wages.[4] Given this inequitable scenario, labor as a single factor has assumed unprecedented importance and emphasis, and the independent trade union movement is emerging as a powerful force in the struggle for a democratic South Africa.

1973 proved to be a particularly crucial year for labor relations in South Africa when waves of strikes swept throughout Natal. This significant and substantial labor unrest represented but another wave of dissatisfaction on the part of black workers.[5] Only when crisis conditions prevailed did the state acknowledge the need for some kind of 'reform', hence the restructuring and overhauling of the labor relations system beginning towards the end of the decade.[6] Many factors accounted for the industrial turbulence that prevailed; the most notable being the unprecedented growth of independent black and non-racial trade unions which was a spin-off in part of the progressive urbanization of the black population,[7] the relatively higher levels of education and the increasing employment of blacks in higher skilled positions. The business community in the meantime acknowledged that there were simply not enough whites to maintain the high rate of growth regarded as necessary and vital to the country's development.[8]

Historically registered trade unions (representing predominantly white workers) have been able to consolidate their political position, negotiate for wage increases, and generally improve working and living standards through participation in the industrial council system (bodies on which both organized workers and employers are represented). The industrial councils represent a developed industrial relations system based on the partnership of registered trade unions and employers. Until relatively recently, black and non-racial unions were excluded from the industrial council system. Legislation legalizing these unions was introduced in 1979 which provided the opportunity for participation in the industrial council system.

Previously, black workers were excluded from the definition 'employee' in the Industrial Conciliation Act. This created a dualistic structure of industrial relations; a legalistic, formal guarantee of certain industrial rights to white, some 'colored' and Indian workers and a repressive framework for African workers embodied in the Black Labor Relations Regulation Act No. 48 of 1953[9] [now repealed]. Moreover, African workers were restricted in upward and geophical mobility by the job reservation clause and the mechanisms of the system of influx control.

The operation of the Black (Urban Areas) Consolidation Act No. 25 of 1945 and other discriminatory legislation maintains an insuperable barrier between black and white workers, forcing blacks into manual, lower-paying labor (where jobs are available) and creating an abundant supply of cheap labor housed in the bantustans.

Influx control is inextricably bound to the questions of citizenship and land-ownership. Shortly after the formation of the Union of South Africa in 1910, the Native Lands Act No. 27 of 1913 was passed, setting aside 7 percent of the total land mass of South Africa for ownership and occupancy by the black population. That amount was increased to 13.5 percent with the passage of the Development Trust and Land Act No. 18 of 1936. Black people are not allowed to own land in the 'white' areas of South Africa.[10]

The 13.5 percent of the land allocated for black occupation comprise scattered fragments of land, designated as the 'Homelands' for the country's black population. With the exception of Bophutatswana, these bantustans lack exploitable minerals and offer poor prospects for agriculture. The bantustant system is closely linked with the government's recent policy of forcibly removing settled black communities from the 'white' areas of South Africa to remote regions of the bantustans. This mass-eviction forces families to try and eke out a living in a sparse and desolate wasteland, where survival escapes possibility.

The right of black people to be in the 'white' areas is regulated by the influx control system, which is embedded in the Black (Urban Areas) Consolidation Act No. 25 of 1945. Control is exercised through Section 10 of the Act, which contains a general prohibition against black persons being in an urban area for longer than 72 hours. To qualify under Section 10 requires proof of continuous residence since birth; continuous employment by the same employer for ten years, or continuous residence for fifteen years; being the wife or dependent child of one qualified due to continued residence or employment; or permission from the local labor bureau.

Black people who remain in an urban area without authorization risk a fine of R100 ($70) and/or three months imprisonment. It is mandatory for all black South Africans over the age of sixteen to carry a reference book ('pass') at all times. The pass contains a photograph, fingerprints and other information serving to identify the holder. Without passes, black people cannot work, obtain housing, register births, or obtain the rights oulined in Section 10.

Foreign blacks[11] have no rights to live or work in South Africa. Their presence in South Africa is dependent entirely upon permission which may be granted or refused in an arbitrary manner, and, once permission is granted, can be withdrawn without any reason given.

Citizenship in such territories depends on ethnic origin, birth in an 'independent bantustan' and sometimes even such tenuous links as cultural affinity or language, and not necessarily on residence, domicile or choice of the individual concerned. In April of 1984, the South African government passed the Aliens and Immigration Laws Amendment Act, which alters some of the laws covering these 'foreigners'. The significance of these amendments must be seen in light of the citizenship provisions of the Black (Urban Areas) Consolidation Act (outlined above).

The amendments provide for a fine of R5,000 or two years' imprisonment for anyone employing or harboring an 'illegal alien' and a fine of R500 for failing to produce on demand the necessary permit needed to enter South Africa.

Officers of the South African state guard against Section 10 offenses vigorously. Raids are conducted regularly on men's hostels, servants' quarters and places generally populated by black urban dwellers. For example, in 1982, 206,022 black people were arrested for alleged contravention of Section 10 requirements.[12]

The position of the ruling white government in South Africa has always been contradictory vis-à-vis the presence of black people in the 'white' areas. On the one hand, the official ideology reflects a desire to maintain the number of black residents in the city at a minimum, while conversely requiring the presence of blacks in the cities to keep industry and commerce serviced, and to maintain productivity at an optimum level. In other words, the system of influx control serves a contradictory purpose: to control the number of black people who come to the white areas so that their numbers do not reach 'unacceptable' levels, while at the same time requiring sufficient numbers in order to maintain a cheap and constant supply of labor to serve the needs of industry and commerce.[13]

Various mechanisms have been utilized to increasingly exclude black people from the 'white areas' and narrowing or removing the rights of people to be there while simultaneously developing administrative processes in order to channel the movement of labor to the cities.

However, since 1979, when the Industrial Conciliation Act was amended to allow the incorporation of black and non-racial unions into the formal legal labor relations structures, the imperative of the 'new labor dispensation' seemed to be somewhat at odds with the requirements of the influx control system. The development of a fair and equitable employment jurisprudence by the industrial court intrinsically carries with it an armory of rights for workers which differ starkly from the erosion of rights manifested in the system of influx control. In fact, this conflict is particularly apparent in issues involving job security, where the industrial court has held that there is a right to security of employment. This right is grounded in the concept of an unfair labor practice and provides workers with a very real weapon to use against employers whose actions might result in not only loss of employment, but also the right to reside in 'white' areas.

The dimensions of this apparent conflict in apartheid ideology and the very concrete problems it presents for tranquil labor relations is yet difficult to gauge. Suffice to say that rights gained in the workplace can only serve to undermine or erode the absence of those rights outside the workplace.

That South Africa is often embraced within the arena of the international democratic order by certain of her economic allies, does not detract from the reality of her omission to subscribe to most of the principles embodied in the political structures of the majority of democratic governments, most notably the universal franchise. Black workers operate under legislation which is a denial of the rule of law as traditionally understood and accepted in democratic countries. The legislation that exists serves primarily to protect the interests of white workers.

Therefore, the absence of a democratic political order to a large extent vitiates against the establishment of a democratic industrial system of labor relations. Negotiations are not simply about wages and conditions of employment, but they spill over into the place of the black worker in the wider South African society.

Circumstances have forced black workers to carve out a niche for themselves as a class, and this class has further attempted through various means at its disposal to extract, despite great opposition from both management and the state, certain benefits which have been hard fought for and won in the international labor community.

A lengthy discussion of the South African social, economic and political scenario has been excluded from this paper for reasons of brevity. Suffice to say that in its embryonic stage the emerging independent trade union movement found itself in a hostile environment. It found as its opposition a formidable alliance between the South African state and the employers.

A combination of tactics like flatly refusing recognition of unions, to forcing majority unions to bargain at plant-level together with minority unions (a clear violation of the principle of majority unionism), to employers using strikes as an opportunity to indulge in 'union bashing' were utilized to slow down or jeopardize the growth of what was perceived as militant black trade unionism. These activities on the part of management very often coincided with harassment on the part of the South African state. All kinds of pernicious strategies were adopted by the South African government to penalize the new unions. These strategies ranged from charging unions with running 'unregistered funeral societies' when they offered small funeral benefits to raids on their offices by security policemen under a variety of pretexts. Some factories even had organizers arrested outside their premises, claiming they were 'obstructing the pavement'. In June 1980, the Minister of Health, Welfare and Pensions used Section 29 of the Fund Raising Act of 1980 to cut off the Federation of South African Trade Union's right to raise funds inside or outside the country.

However, depsite these dismal beginnings, the independent trade union movement managed to weather the storm. By 1977 the South African government finally acknowledged that a powerful, cohesive independent trade union movement was to be inextricably linked to the industrial system and a Commission was appointed to investigate South Africa's archaic and inadequate labor legislation.

This Commission and its later recommendations represented a new era of 'reform' on the part of the South African state. This attempt at reform of the racial division of labor and all its inequitable manifestation represent one significant point, *viz.*, that it is not in the interests of the capitalist class that such division be maintained.

Firstly, it is acknowledged that South Africa has experienced, for the last two decades, at least, a severe shortage of skilled labor.

This shortage is a direct spin-off from an inferior educational system for black and job color bar regulations which have become the preoccupation of the white trade unions. This has been coupled with a slow growth rate of the white population, or rather a growth rate not consonant with the requirements of capital. This situation has endured despite the recession of recent years.

The business community in South Africa have, therefore, embarked on an energetic crusade to change this pattern and stave off or significantly reduce the shortage of skilled labor.[14] This is not to suggest the imperative to modify the racist division of labor in South Africa resulted purely from an acknowledgment of the shortage of skilled labor. Rather, such modification became imperative for the business sector after assessing the total picture of the prevailing economic crisis and political strife, particularly in the form of black urban struggles in Soweto and other major metropolitan centers. The total scenario presented by this crisis has become more of a concern because of reduced profits. Whereas, the sixties and early seventies was a boom era in South Africa, political turbulence has become a major factor in the diminished profitability which so pervades the economic arena.[15]

The need to restore profit levels and alleviate the economic crisis therefore becomes entwined with the political aspirations of South Africa's disenfranchised majority black population. A compromise from the point of view of the business sector class would have to coincide with the demands of the black population, particularly the working class.[16]

The need to restore the lush economic environment for the owners of capital in South Africa has also brought to the fore the ideological warfare occurring within its boundaries. In a nutshell, the political and economic crisis has shaken the ideological foundations of the free enterprise system in South Africa.[17]

Recognising the permanence and potential strength of the black and non-racial trade union movement, attempts have been made to distinguish between 'political' and 'economic' issues — the implication being that economic issues are appropriate ones to be pursued by trade unions.

The attempt to distinguish, for example, between bus boycotts or rent boycotts on the one hand, and struggles for higher wages on the other, as falling within political or economic camps masks the reality. Where the system has imposed conditions which so persistently reinforce oppression at all levels, the struggle of the working class exists as a fusion of economic and political interests, and to make arbitrary distinctions escapes the point. The South African labor statute prohibits political activities on the part of trade unions — but this prohibition has not served as the deterrent that it was intended to be.[18]

Within the independent, non-racial and black trade union movement there is a continuing and often heated debate as to the links with community organizations and to what extent the unions should take up political issues. Certain trade unions (and this position was represented most visibly by the Federation of South African Trade Unions and the General Workers Union) saw the need to build strength in the workplace in order to confront the other aspects of apartheid outside the workplace from a position of strength. They also see participation in overtly political action as inviting the wrath of the South African state repressive machinery. The other view, represented most visibly by MACWUSA and SAAWU, argued that black workers' problems cannot be artificially divided into 'industrial' and 'political' sections, since those problems are both direct results of apartheid policies. These unions hold the view that links with community organizations actually increase their potential strength. Sisa Njikelana encapsulates this posture:

> 'The distinction between trade union struggles and struggles engaged in by other mass organizations has tended to be exaggerated in an attempt to show that the economic struggles waged by the unions are far more real and working class in nature than other mass based struggles'.[19]

> 'Are workers' struggles for higher wages that unrelated to or bus boycotts? Even those community and other struggles which are not so clearly economically based, such as those waged in the schools for a free and better education system, are issues which directly affect the working class. These issues link the community based and often more political struggles directly to the economic struggles being waged by the unions'.[20]

However, these differences of strategy were to some extent eroded during November 1984, when a broad-based coalition of trade unions combined their united strength in a highly successful stay-away, which involved between 300,000 and 800,000 workers, making it the largest in South African history. The only other work stoppage of significant importance related to trade union unified strategy, and in the last few years occurred after the death of Neil Agget in police detention in 1982. The death of Neil Agget provided the trade union movement with the opportunity of exhibiting their united strength. The work stoppage was of historical significance, since it was the first time that nation-wide industrial action was utilized at the point of production in support of a political demand. The event was significant, too, in that it demonstrated the potentially mobilizing ability of the independent trade union movement, who had succeeded in uniting over 1,000,000 workers nation-wide in the space of two days.

In South Africa, as is the case in many countries where labor attempts to flex its muscles in the face of oppressive governments, it is a truism that the shop floor becomes a political forum. The workplace provides an atmosphere for prolonged homogeneous affiliation. It is the one place where all aspiration (economic and political) will coalesce, and where all dimensions of the wide political struggle can be streamlined and placed in focus.

As the urban black population increases in number, with aspirations soaring upward, the potential of this group cannot be ignored. In the final analysis a glaring contrast between unfair conditions outside the workplace and growing integration and assimilation in the industrial sector will further exacerbate tensions already existing, and an acceptable solution is vital. In the absence of any meaningful political structures within which black workers are able to exert their influence on national policy, recourse will be taken more frequently to strike action, boycotts, and other economic weapons at their disposal.

The alliances which emerged in late 1983, in response to the South African government's imposition of a new constitutional framework, between trade unions and popular 'community' organizations have been interpreted as a new phase of resistance to apartheid.

'Workers movements are becoming increasingly sophisticated. They understand the need to get more involved in community issues and to use their strength on the factory floor to resolve these community issues'.[21]

Community issues are not separated completely from work-related issues. Alec Erwin of the Federation of South African Trade Unions puts it succinctly:

'Low wages in South Africa are associated with the fundamental inequities of our society — racial discrimination, influx control, the migrant labor system, the appropriate of black land, the destruction of black agriculture and the suppression of trade unions. Inevitably, therefore, better wages becomes a political demand and workers do not confine their perception of wages to the narrow economics of their particular factory'.[22]

The formation of one labor federation in South Africa, *viz.* the Congress of South African Trade Unions, largely renders the debate within trade union circles regarding community involvement moot at this point, since the new federation will obviously take position on that very issue. Most importantly, the political versus economic distinction is being made redundant by the practices of the South African government itself, since in the last few months it has brought all the might of its repressive apparatus against all strata of society — women, children and workers. And trade unions wishing to slavishly adhere to workplace issues will find themselves more and more out of line with their membership. As Alec Erwin stated after the Transvaal Stayway:

'Our attitude is clear. If something affects our organization and our members, we will respond'.[23]

The formation of the Congress of South African Trade Unions is a milestone in South Africa's labor history. As the conflict grows, and the tentacular state repression touches more lives, labor's muscle will require flexing — the outcome escapes prediction at this stage.

Notes

1. This paper does not mention the South African Congress of Trade Unions (SACTU) since it concentrates on trade union developments after 1973. This does not suggest that SACTU does and has not played a vital role in labor issues in South Africa. However, SACTU operates under a different set of conditions and circumstances, since it was forced into exile in the early 1960s. The scope of this paper does not allow an analysis of external developments in the form of the SACTU international solidarity network, but instead attempts to analyse developments within South Africa. For an in-depth study of SACTU struggles and victories see Luckhart, Ken, and Brenda Wall, *Working for Freedom*, as well as *Organise. . . or Starve* by the same authors.

2. South African labor legislation has ensured that 'the white workers have come to form an aristocracy of labor consisting of skilled and supervisory workers, most of whom enjoy a high degree of privilege and join with their employers in policing the exploitation of natives'. Rex, J 'The Plural Society: The South African Case' *Race* Vol. XI No. 4 1971. The passage of the Industrial Conciliation Act of 1924 offered white workers a range of economic benefits based on racial privilege.

3. This clause empowered the Minister of Labor to reserve any job for whites. The enactment of this section was merely a continuation of the 'industiral color bar' which originated in the exploitative conditions of the mining industry.

4. *South Africa Fact Sheet* Africa Fund, New York (1984).

5. Black workers have, since the turn of the century and particularly after industrialization took root in South Africa, rejected the persistently exploitative and repressive system to which they were subjected. Such rejection repeatedly culminated in widespread strikes. For example, the significant strike by 100,000 African mineworkers at twenty-one mines in 1946 was brutally crushed by the South African police, who killed twelve strikers and injured 1,200. See Luckhart, Ken, and Brenda Wall *Working for Freedom*, World Council of Churches, Geneva (1981). See also Murray, Martin J (ed.)

South African Capitalism and Black Political Opposition Schenkman Publishing Co., Cambridge, Massachusetts (1982).

6. Between January and the end of March 1973, more than one hundred and sixty strikes involving in excess of 61,000 workers occurred in Durban. One of the union officials involved stated:

 'The mass strikes in the Natal province demonstrated the unity of the black working class across divisions between migrant and urban workers, between different industries, and even between industiral and agricultural workers. . . Employers and the police responded by threatening mass dismissals and prosecutions and eventually offering some minor wage increases. . . The momentum of the strike was ultimately broken through the growing presence of the police in army uniforms flown in from other centres, and the lack of strike funds. Despite the relatively small wage increases. . . the consciousness of the workers had advanced considerably beyond the relative caution of the period of repression before the strikes. . . .'

 Luckhart, Ken, and Brenda Wall *Organize . . . or Starve! The History of the South African Congress of Trade Unions.* International Publishers, New York, (1980) [p. 449]. In addition to labor unrest, a wave of urban unrest hit South Africa in 1976 involving workers in a series of 'stay-aways' as part of the wider political protests.

7. Despite official attempts through 'pass' laws and inadequate housing to relocate black people to the bantustans, large numbers moved to the city (sometimes illegally) in search for jobs. The proliferation of squatter communities outside the major metropolitan areas is a visible manifestation of this trend. As rural areas become more impoverished and are unable to provide for 'surplus' people within their boundaries, the situation will worsen.

8. These sentiments were reiterated in the Wiehahn Commission Report.

9. The Act made provision for a system of in-plant bargaining through works and liaison committees. Agreements reached by these committees, although binding on employers and employees who are party to the agreement, would not have the same legal force as Industrial council agreements. Moreover,

no provision was made for legal sanctions in the vent of non-compliance. These committee structures in no way represented the intrinsic power of an independent trade union and, in fact, fell far short of the aspirations of workers to negotiate their conditions of employment. Quite clearly, the lack of effective participation by African workers in industrial council decisions which affect them are apparent. So too are the confusing effect which committee agreements could have in industries where industrial council agreements apply. The Act provided for representation of both employers and employees on liaison committees. Obviously, such a situation vitiates against independent decision-making since the unequal bargaining position of the worker is reflected in the liaison committee.

10. These areas generally comprise all of the cities, most industrial and commercial complexes, farmlands and the mining areas.

11. These are citizens of neighboring states like Botswana, Swaziland, Mozambique, Lesotho and Malawi, who provide labor for the mines.

12. See Annual Survey; South African Institute of Race Relations 1982.

13. For an excellent discussion and analysis of this contradiction see Budlende, Geoff 'Incorporation and Exclusion: Recent Developments in Labor Law and Influx Control' in *South African Journal of Human Rights*, Vol. 1 Part 1 May 1985, pp. 3–9.

14. See, *e.g.*, statement by E. Leistner of the African Institute: '. . . a white monopoly of highly skilled and responsible posts in business administration. . . was no longer tenable. Members of other racial groups would have to move up into such positions if economic growth rates were not to fall to even lower levels. Research has shown that within fifteen years at least 500,000 white clerical jobs would be vacant unless other races were trained to fill work gaps vital for industrial expansion'. South African Institute for Race Relations, *Survey of Race Relations* (1976), p. 291.

15. *Id*. After the political lull of the 1960's, a direct result of the South African government's banning of the most important resistance movements, its enforced exile and incarceration of popular leaders like Nelson Mandela, Walter Sisulu and Robert

Subukwe, among others, resistance against government policy reached unprecedented heights during the 1970s. The wave of strikes commencing in 1973, followed by the mass uprising in 1976 and student protests in 1980 shook the hitherto steadfast foundations of apartheid ideology. This combined industrial and political unrest caused consternation in the upper echelons of government and business. These activities continue to the present.

16. The militancy and organization of this class, as evidenced in the development and growth of the black and non-racial trade union movement, vitiates the possibility of further assaults on their working conditions. The risk of even greater economic and political instability which might result is very real for the capitalists.

17. See, for example, the statement of Dr. S.P. Du Toit Viljoen of the 'Free Market Foundation', as it appeared in the *Financial Mail* after the 1976 Soweto uprising: 'There is a general tendency for young Africans to be anti-free enterprise'. *Id.*, February 11, 1977, p. 376.

18. Strikes of solidarity, general stay-aways to protect rent increases and school conditions, alignment with popular political movements on the part of the independent trade union movement all fly in the face of this proscription.

19. Nijkelana S. 'Unions and the U.D.F.', *Work in Progress* [p. 32].

20. *Id.*

21. Statement of Dr. Duncan Innes of the University of Witwatersand in *The Star*, February 21, 1984.

22. Erwin, Alec 'The Remuneration Package: A Survival or Living Wage', *Industrial Relations Journal of South Africa*, Vol. 3, No. 1, 1983, p. 54.

23. *Id.*

PEACE AND SECURITY IN SOUTHERN AFRICA: THE ROLE OF LIBERATION MOVEMENTS

Hamisi S. Kibola
Lecturer in International Law, Centre for Foreign Relations,
Dar es Salaam

Introduction

In terms of appraising the situation in the region, the Second International Conference on Peace and Security in Southern Africa comes at an appropriate moment. In the first place, the conference comes at a time when the international community has dedicated 1986 the International Year of Peace. Secondly, the conference comes about one month after the fall of Leabua Jonathan's Government in South African locked Lesotho. Thirdly, the conference has come at a point when events in the region clearly point towards one direction — that, in spite of South Africa's manifest military and economic superiority, its capacity to control effectively violent as well as non-violent opposition from the majority population within South Africa and Namibia has its limits.

The situation inside South Africa and Namibia has developed progressively from one of isolated attacks on the apartheid regime's economic and security installations to a consistent and comprehensive set of both coordinated as well as spontaneous measures against the regime. The majority of the people are up against the racist regime. They are continuously manifesting a common hatred against it.

South Africa's strategy of undermining liberation movements at home and destabilizing Front Line States (FLS) offering refuge to their combatants has not fully delivered the goods. It has managed to stifle open military support in favor of liberation movements, as the cases of Mozambique and Angola have demonstrated, but this is quite far from its intentions of 'stamping' out the activities of liberation movements both in the FLS as well as within South Africa and Namibia.

This paper puts forward what are considered to be the necessary conditions which must be brought into play before peace and security can be achieved in the region, with specific reference to the role of liberation movements. Peace and security are not questions which can be taken for granted. They are controversial issues. In this paper, reference to them should be taken to mean the establishment of those conditions which are necessary for the attainment of social and economic development for the benefit and in the interest of the people of the region. Attention should also be focused on peace and security not as ends in themselves, but rather as the means for the continuation of politics by peaceful means. The question succintly put is: what conditions are necessary before the politics of peace can determine the developmental question in the region?

This paper first discusses recent major problems that have distinguished the struggle in South Africa and Namibia from that which was waged in the neighboring FLS before independence (e.g. Mozambique and Zimbabwe). These developments are very likely to affect the political as well as the military strategy of liberation movements in the two countries. The assumptions and contentions which underlie the role to be attributed to liberation movements, both generally as well as specifically in relation to the aforementioned problems, are then discussed. It is pointed out that armed struggle was imposed upon the people of South Africa and Namibia, as was the case with a large number of other peoples who have fought for their self-determination. This has been done for the very simple reason that it provides a sound basis for the assessment of the role of liberation movements in the very painful problems of instability in Southern Africa.

Complexity of the Southern Africa situation in the light of recent events

Recent events in Southern Africa have demonstrated the degree of complexity which surrounds the situation in the region. Of course, the struggle for the liberation of South Africa and Namibia rages on. Whereas the FLS previously offered full support to this struggle, it has now become clear that limits are being forcibly imposed. The RSA is attempting, with all its means, to ensure that proximate external assistance, especially from the FLS, is no longer provided to liberation movements fighting against the apartheid regime.

The RSA has managed to make the conflict regional so that at present the South African and Namibia issues are linked to the Angolan, Mozambican and Lesothos' problems. At the same time as the RSA maintains a stronghold within the country, Namibian independence is made conditional upon Cuban withdrawal from Angola and sometimes to the dismay of many, upon negotiation between MPLA and UNITA.

The complicated set of relations that have emerged now presents a pattern whereby one can identify, among others, three significant levels of interaction; firstly, the struggle by liberation movements inside South Africa and Namibia; secondly, relations between RSA and FLS who have not only a moral, but also a formal obligation (i.e., from the point of view of OAU liberation strategy) to assist liberation movements; and thirdly, relations between liberation movements and the FLS which, in spite of all the complications, still remain intimate. These three levels of interaction relate to each other and, judging from recent developments, the second has significantly affected the others. The FLS finds in South Africa both an enemy as well as enforced partnership. They are against the apartheid regime, but they have to exist with it.

Considered from the above scenario, the position of liberation movements becomes very precarious. The OAU liberation strategy, in which the role of liberation movements could be fixed for instance, comes under test. What should be the response of the liberation movements? The following assumptions and contentions set the pace for the conclusions derived in this paper.

Assumptions and contentions

Any analysis of the topic hereby covered will have to take as its starting point one fundamental assumption — that *the struggle being waged by liberation movements in South Africa and Namibia is a struggle for peace* and, conversely, that opposition by the apartheid regime to this struggle is aimed at maintaining a status quo of domination, oppression and intimidation of the South African and Namibian people, as well as the peoples of the neighboring FLS. Opposition to the liberation struggle therefore constitutes the primary threat to peace and security in the region.

From this assumption, several contentions flow;

(a) That, as such, the struggle being waged by Liberation Movements in the Republic of South Africa (RSA) and Namibia is a legitimate struggle;
(b) That liberation movements should be viewed as positive contributors to the desired process of pacification and stabilization in Southern Africa rather that its detractors;
(c) That any initiative aimed at bringing about peace and enhancing security in Southern Africa must involve the participation of liberation movements — if this crucial consideration is ignored, in favor of heavy handedness, any such initiative is likely to be nullified by history; and
(d) That therefore, in the complicated pattern of existing relations, ways should be found to give liberation movements maximum opportunities to play an active and effective role in the movement towards peace and security in the region.

This paper argues that the reality of all these propositions is evident in the very recent events that have been unfolding in the region. In the first place, the legitimacy of the struggle waged by liberation movements in South Africa and Namibia is now getting on South African nerves. Gone are the days when opposition to the apartheid regime could simply be regarded as 'terrorist'. The RSA must come to grips with the fact that it cannot characterize a majority of its population as terrorists. The real terrorist is now clearly known. It is the minority apartheid regime of South Africa.

Secondly, recent symbolic contacts between the African National Congress of South Africa (ANC) and various interest groups from South Africa demonstrate the extent to which this movement is interested in exploiting the potential of various avenues for the purpose of stabilizing the general situation in the country and elsewhere in the region. These contacts, which are essentially tactical, also demonstrate the constructive role which the ANC is prepared to play, in spite of being intimidated by the apartheid regime. *Per se* the contacts may appear insignificant, but considered together with other events taking place currently they cannot be easily ignored.

Thirdly, it has now become evident that partial peace initiatives with the RSA have minimum prospects of success so long as apartheid persists in South Africa. Although this cannot be attributed to the apparent neglect of the positions of the liberation movements involved, none can deny that the process of partial peace has been unsuccessful and eventually quite painful to those involved.

Liberation and peace

Apartheid and colonialism are both vitiated in the present international system. In common parlance, apartheid has become characterized as 'a crime against humanity'. Apartheid and colonialism have been condemned by the international community at large. Yet in South Africa the racist regime insists on maintaining apartheid. Namibia has been colonized and illegaally occupied. Furthermore, South Africa has applied and continues to apply apartheid in the territory.

There can be no peace in Southern Africa unless the process of national liberation in South Africa and Namibia takes its natural course. Basic to this contention is the fact that apartheid and colonialism are not compatible with peace and security, neither in Southern Africa nor in any other part of the world. Within the context of Southern Africa, only self-determination of the oppressed peoples can be reconciled with peace in the region and can create conditions for its realization.

The right to self-determination of the South African and Namibian peoples is presently disputed by only one Government in the world — the Government of the racist Republic of South Africa (RSA). Even South Africa's imperialist allies do not challenge this right, though they assist the republic in its violation. This sacred and fundamental right has been enshrined in the Charter of the United Nations, to which the RSA is formally a party, but whose principles it is more inclined to ignore than to observe. The UN Charter commits the organization to 'develop friendly relations among nations based on respects for the principle of equal rights and self determination of peoples'. However, the RSA turns a blind eye to this quite important commitment.

Apart from the UN Charter, the right to self-determination has been reiterated in countless resolutions of the UN General Assembly. As a political necessity and juridical reality, the right to self-determination is evident. Yet, the South African and Namibian peoples have been forcibly denied this basic human right and their claims to enjoy it have been viewed as either communist or terrorist maneuvres, thereby 'legitimising' (sic) the strategy of South Africa and its allies of inciting super power 'mongery' in Southern Africa. The peoples of South Africa and Namibia thus continue to suffer together with those of the neighboring FLS, who have to face consistent aggression from the South African Defence Force (SADF).

In South Africa, the apartheid regime set aside 87% of its land for a white minority and left the remaining 13% for the majority black population. Blacks have been banished in Bantustans with promises of independence which have no prospect of safeguarding the interests of South African people. The territorial integrity of South African is being violated. South Africans face massive denationalization with the alternative of belonging to Bantustans, some of which have more than half of their food imported, more than 50% of their population unemployed and 40% of their rural population landless. The apartheid regime continues to establish and maintain conditions for the poverty and weakness of the South African people so that they remain hopelessly doomed to oppression and exploitation.

Much could be said about the evils of the apartheid system in South Africa. Apartheid's land tenure, education system, health policy etc. are all directed towards the nourishment of a minority and the neglect of the majority. The agricultural and mineral resources of South Africa, which should have been used for the benefit of the South African poeple, have been put at the exclusive disposal of the white minority and multinationals from Western countries. Apartheid should be understood not only as a system of racial discrimination, but also as a tool for the exploitation and oppression of the majority in South Africa.

In *Namibia*, the RSA clings to its illegal occupation. It has entrenched the apartheid system there as well as now has a vested interested in its existence, since a failure in the territory will obviously be linked to the struggle taking place inside South Africa. Green and Kiljunen have vividly summarized the violence that has characterized South Africa's rule over the territory.

'There is the theft of land which has made the African people unable to subsist in their "reserves" and left only one choice, to work or to starve. There is the contract labor system which breaks up families and makes possible wages below family subsistence because dependents are left in the reserves. There is the systematic seizure, by force, by law and by administrative devices, of most of the usable land, virtually all of the water and all of the mineral and fishing rights'.

South African and various other corporations from a select group of Western countries continue to plunder the natural wealth and resources of the country unheeded. Despite being inhabitants of one of the richest countries in Africa in terms of natural wealth and resources, the people of Namibia find themselves overwhelmed by poverty imposed from outside.

The people of South Africa and Namibia have no obligation to remain exploited and oppressed. On the contrary, they have the right to the restoration of their dignity and respect as human beings, as well as the right to determine their own destiny. Apartheid and colonialism are in themselves inherently violent. As already argued therefore, there can be no peace in Southern Africa until such time as these evils against mankind have been dismantled. *To argue for peace in Southern Africa without liberation is to follow a dark alley which has no prospect of leading into something meaningful.* It would have been different if the RSA could have been convinced to dismantle apartheid by peaceful means, but as the following paragraphs show, this is definitely not the case.

Peaceful initiatives by liberation movements and imposed armed struggle

The history of the colonization of the African continent is characterized by violence against the African people. African forefathers heroically resisted colonial rule. They were defeated, but continuously challenged colonial authorities by massive uprisings until such time as colonial superiority became dominant. In South Africa, the Bambata uprising signalled the end of early resistance. When the Herero resistance came to an end in 1907 the Germans were victorious. It left the Herero tribe 'vastly diminished with only some 15,000 starving refugees remaining'. The same could be said of other parts of Africa where early resistance came to an end for various reasons ranging from the superiority of colonial weaponry to frictions among African feudal establishments. Isolated uprisings still took place but granted colonial superiority, they were not likely to shake up the colonial establishment.

The wars of liberation that brought independence to Mozambique, Angola, Zimbabwe and other parts of Africa were indeed a continuation of the aforementioned early resistance, if only because colonial conquest did not bring with it an end to the spirit of African independence. The wars of national liberation, however, took place only when it became crystal clear that colonial and racist regimes were not sensitive to peaceful initiatives aimed at ending colonization or racism. The cases of Mozambique, Angola, South Africa and Namibia demonstrate the reality of this view. In all these countries, petitions, strikes, demonstrations as well as boycotts of a purely non-violent character were invoked. Literary works were also used as a means of expressing opposition to colonial and racist rule.

In Mozambique, poetry, the organization of cooperatives, strikes and demonstrations expressed opposition to Portuguese rule. In 1947, 1956 and 1963, for instance, the then Laurenco Marques dockyard was the scene of strikes by dockworkers. Beira and Nacala dockers joined their colleagues of Laurenco Marques in 1963. In the countryside, demonstrations against colonial rule also took place. These and similar peaceful protests against Portuguese colonialism were met with heavy police repression resulting in a number of deaths and sometimes full scale massacres.

Political agitation, manifestos, clandestine organizations through cells, work stoppages, refusal to pay taxes as well as demonstrations also featured in the early phase of the liberation struggle in Angola. Similarly, these were met with initially police and later military repression.

When in 1960, for instance, the people in Neto's home area demanded his release from prison, Portuguese troops responded by opening fire on them, killing thirty and injuring about two hundred of them.

The same story can be repeated in the case of Namibia. Strikes demonstrations, boycotts and petitions were invoked. In reply, public meetings were banned and detention without due process made the order of the day. Many people were killed and injured in the process of suppressing what was evidently quite peaceful opposition.

In South Africa, the peaceful initiative came to an end with the massacres at Sharpeville and Langa where many people were murdered in cold blood for having participated in peaceful demonstrations. The banning of ANC and PAC thereafter and their movement underground sounded the hopelessness of peaceful struggle against the apartheid regime. As argued by Gibson:

'Non violent protest was repressed with such violence on the part of the white regime that recourse to violence by Africans seems more a measure of self defence and survival than arbitrary defiance of an unjust but peaceful order'.

In all the above-mentioned cases, the decision to adopt armed struggle was therefore not an option. It was imposed by the oppressive regimes in power. This was evident in the facts established on the ground and was reflected in speeches of leaders of liberation movements as well as resolutions of various international forms.

Sam Nujoma, leader of the South West Africa Peoples organization, SWAPO, went on record as having said that:

'It was after all our efforts to reach a peaceful solution had resulted in a stalemate, that my organization decided to embark upon armed resistance as the only remaining means open to us. The decision to initiate armed resistance is by no means an easy one, and I for one was at pains to agree to such a decision, but when my people have said "enough" it is enough'.

The Heads of States and the Government of the East and Central African States twice made clear their position on the only viable means of achieving African liberation in the South. In the Lusaka manifesto, they defined the objectives of liberation and stated:

'We have always preferred and we still prefer, to achieve it without physical violence. We would prefer to negotiate rather than destroy, to talk rather than kill. We do not advocate violence; we advocate an end to the violence against human dignity which is now being perpetrated by the oppressors of Africa. If peaceful progress to emancipation were possible, or if changed circumstances were to make it possible, in the future, we would urge our brothers in the resistance movement to use peaceful methods of struggle even at the cost of some compromise on the timing of change. But while peaceful progress is blocked by actions of those at present in power in the states of Southern Africa we have no choice but to give the peoples of those territories all the support of which we are capable in the struggle against their oppressors'.

The Lusaka Manifesto was adopted about seventeen years ago. The Manifesto was further confirmed by the OAU and thereafter presented to the UN General Assembly where it was made a UN document. The truth of the Manifesto is borne out by the fact that, since then, every state which has gained independence in Southern Africa has only been able to do so through armed struggle. Evidently, the Manifesto's thesis is even truer now, given the intransigence characteristic of the RSA's position inside the republic as well as in Namibia. The righteousness of the wars of national liberation in Southern Africa is also clear from UN resolutions. In 1975, for instance, the UN strongly reaffirmed 'The legitimacy of the struggle of the oppressed people of South Africa and their liberation movements, *by all possible means* for the seizure of power by the people and the exercise of their inalienable right of self determination'. Since then, this reaffirmation has been repeated regularly.

Further non-violent action: the onus is on South Africa

The dominant liberation movements in South Africa and Namibia have thus been forced to adopt armed struggle as the only viable way in which they could restore the birthright of their peoples. Nevertheless, this should not mean that they have abandoned the alternative non-violent avenue of realizing their objectives, namely, negotiation. No doubt exists, however, that this has been viewed as a secondary means, leaving armed struggle as primary for that purpose.

In South Africa, the apartheid regime has closed all avenues of negotiation claiming that any movement interested in change in the country should in the first place renounce violence as a means of effecting change. The regime is therefore blind to its own violence and is only interested in doing away with the counter violence that it has incited. The liberation movements of South Africa are not against peaceful change through negotiations 'if this were possible'.

The Namibian situation demonstrates vividly Pretoria's negative attitude towards the possibility of a negotiated settlement, showing clearly that its intentions are more to delay the process of change than to bring an end to its illegal occupation there.

SWAPO is one of the parties which took part in the consultative process carried out under the auspices of the 'Contact Group' of five Western countries. In the first quarter of 1978, the group put forward a 'Proposal for a Settlement in Namibia', containing major factors of agreement. This proposal was submitted to the Security Council of the United Nations and actually formed a basis for a UN Plan for the Independence of Namibia. It was adopted as UN Security Council Resolution 435 of 1978. The main elements of this plan included a ceasefire, restriction of

South African and Namibian forces to base and a phased withdrawal of South African forces from Namibia during which time elections would be held. A United Nations Transitional Assistance Group (UNTAG) was expected to play a crucial role in ensuring that the various elements of the plan were adhered to.

South Africa's sincerity towards the whole process of negotiation faltered as soon as the plan was adopted. Instead of implementing the letter and spirit of Resolution 435, South Africa adopted delaying tactics by raising extraneous and irrelevant issues. Political accommodation of Savimbi, as well as the withdrawal of Cuban troops from Angola were called for.

SWAPO further took the challenge to participate in negotiations aimed at implementing Resolution 435 together with the FLS, internally based parties and South Africa. Early in 1981, SWAPO was among the parties that went to the Geneva talks which ended in vain. South Africa took the opportunity to walk out of the conference and invade the People's Republic of Angola (PRA) immediately thereafter. SWAPO also attended the Lusaka talks convened by the good offices of Zambian President Kenneth Kaunda in May 1984.

In all these negotiations, South Africa's attitude has been that of delaying the genuine process of change in Namibia. Naturally, it sought to protect its own illegitimate interests. Even when a flexible attitude was adopted by the PRA on the linkage of the withdrawal of Cuban forces, RSA maintained its intransigence. Thus the onus surely lies on the apartheid regime to demonstrate that it is interested in the settlement of the question. Namibia's liberation movements cannot carry any blame on their shoulders for the deterioration of the situation. After all, it is not within their competence to withdraw Cuban troops from Angola.

Present setting and some considerations for future action

This paper has attempted to demonstrate the complicated set up of the situation in Southern Africa. The war of national liberation rages on. The apartheid regime of the RSA is intransigent. It has sent its forces across boundaries and invaded the FLS, offering support and refuge to combatants of national liberation movements. It has also mounted economic pressure (at times, blockades) to states supporting national liberation movements. Peace accords, in which the position of liberation movements remain precarious, have been concluded. The question to which analysts of liberation movements in Southern Africa should address themselves is; what is the short term future role of liberation movements in the poltiics of Southern Africa? Should they continue to operate from FLS which will continue to suffer armed invasions from the RSA? To which approach should they devote more attention in this crucial phase of their struggle?

All these questions show that liberation movements still have a tough task ahead of them. This is not to be taken in any way to underate the heroism of the combatants fighting for the self-determination of Namibia and South Africa. As a matter of fact, the military and economic might of the RSA is a force to reckon with. Nevertheless, the success of the liberation struggle is now a foregone conclusion. Victory is certain, but the problem is when it will be achieved. The crucial question is: what can be done to minimize the suffering of the people of Southern Africa at the same time as the struggle for national liberation is intensified.

The reality is that with some exceptions, liberation movements now find it difficult to operate from states bordering the RSA. In response to this recent development, there is only one viable option to be exercised by liberation movements. These have to intensify political mobilization of the broad mass at home and call upon them to revolt against the apartheid regime and as it were, 'make apartheid unworkable'. Liberation movements have already done quite a significant amount of work towards this goal. However, what is called of them is to intensify political mobilization of South Africans and Namibians to the extent that can justify full scale assistance from the FLS with the objective of overthrowing the apartheid regime. The initiative must come from within. Under the circumstances presently existing in Southern Africa, it is useful but not enough to mount raids from the FLS into the RSA. Evidence exists to suggest that the consequences of such raids to both liberation movements as well as the FLS have been quite catastrophic. A general uprising in the RSA will definitely be the strongest guarantee to the FLS that their commitment and substantial overt involvement is justifiable.

At this stage, mention must be made of extraordinary developments that have taken place, particularly inside South Africa since the late seventies. Black Consciousness Movements, Trade Unions, Churches and other anti-apartheid organizations have made such a substantial contribution that the apartheid regime has shown signs of stress. Taking this into consideration the above suggestion of intensified political mobilization inside South Africa simultaneous FLS involvement sounds quite feasible. Liberation movements are more than ever before called upon to organize a common 'Front' and confront the apartheid regime primarily inside South Africa and outside the country.

Conclusion

No doubt the overthrow of the apartheid regime in South Africa and colonialism in Namibia will be instrumental in creating conditions for the continuation of politics by peaceful means in both Namibia and South Africa. The problem is how to overthrow apartheid without causing excessive suffering to the people of Southern Africa, given the very complicated set-up of the region. Old strategies, particularly those based on the traditional role of the FLS, may not necessarily be of any use in solving the present problems. There is a need for liberation movements, the FLS, international organizations and all the peace-loving peoples of the world to face the current complex situation with great inventiveness.

References

1. Gibson, R.; *African Liberation Movements* (Oxford University Press, 1972).
2. Green, R.H. (et al.); *Namibia; The Last Colony* (Longmans 1981).
3. Hastings, A.; *Massacre in Mozambique* (Rex Collings, 1978).
4. Innes, D.; 'Imperialism and the National Struggle in Namibia' *Review of African Political Economy* No. 9 (1978).
5. Coker, C.; 'The South African Elections and Neo-Apartheid' *The World Today* (June 1981).

6. Murray, R. (et al.); *The Role of Foreign Firms in Namibia* Africa Publications Trust, 1974.
7. Spence, J.E.; 'South Africa; Reform Versus Reaction' *The World Today* (Dec. 1981).
8. Spicer, M.; 'Namibia — Elusive Independence' *The World Today* (Oct. 1980).
9. *Apartheid in South Africa and Namibia*, International Commission of Jurists, Geneva, 1974.
10. *A Trust Betrayed*, United Nations, N.Y. 1974.
11. *Namibia, The Facts* International Defence and Aid Fund, London, 1980.
12. *To Be Born A Nation, The Liberation Struggle for Namibia* Department of Information and Publicity, SWAPO of Namibia.
13. Africa Contemporary Records.
14. African Confidential Reports.
15. United Nations Charter.
16. UN General Assembly and Security Council Resolutions.
17. Charter of the Organization of African Unity.
18. Lusaka Manifesto and Mogadisho Declaration.

PROSPECTS FOR NEGOTIATION IN SOUTH AFRICA

Hendrik W. van der Merwe
Director, Centre for Intergroup Studies, University of Cape Town, Rondebosch, Cape Town

Prospects for negotiation in South Africa

The prospects for negotiation in a society torn by conflict such as South Africa are bleak indeed. Noting the obstacles to negotiation between the major contending parties in South Africa, I shall argue that the prospects for negotiation are better than the current state of violence and public rhetoric seem to suggest.

I shall discuss some problems of communication between the major emerging constellations of political-ideological groups — the Establishment and the Extra-Parliamentary opposition — including the violence currently committed by both sides, and the Communist connection of the ANC.

Since this paper deals with negotiation, which is only one aspect of communication between contending parties, and does not discuss or assess the role of pressure, the following points should be stated clearly:

(a) Pressure is required to bring about change in South Africa
(b) Negotiation should not be seen as a substitute for or alternative to pressures for change
(c) Negotiation is therefore a complement to pressure in the communication process.

Conflict is endemic in society

Conflict should not necessarily be seen as bad or destructive. It is endemic in any society and can be seen as stimulating and invigorating. It can serve useful social functions, provided a constructive attitude is projected towards it.

The real problem does not lie in the presence of conflict but in the way it is handled, accommodated and/or resolved. If conflict is handled in a negative, destructive way, it ends in violence, the extreme manifestation of conflict. Violence can serve no long-term constructive social function, even if it may have desirable short-term effects. The extent to which we succeed in the constructive accommodation of conflict, the amount of violence and bloodshed will be reduced.

If we were to be reasonable, we would readily admit in principle (though not easily, in situations where we are personally involved) that conflict, violence and malice could not be attributed to one party only; either to the oppressor or the victim; to the employer or the trade union; to the whites or the blacks. The implication is that we must not anticipate a Utopia under any regime.

The end of apartheid will not mean the end of violence either physical, mental or institutional.

Everyone talks so glibly of the goals of justice and peace as if these are states of society that can be easily achieved. Two years ago, our State President claimed in his New Year's message that South Africa was one of the most peaceful societies in the world, thanks to the protection we receive from the security forces. But Government opponents argue quite the opposite. They believe South Africa is a highly violent society and, in addition, they hold these very security forces responsible for what has become known as institutional or structural violence, i.e. *violence committed by the State* through upholding and enforcing unjust structures and institutions. Many of these critics also imply that the security forces are the only instruments of violence and once we have a new black or non-racial Government there will be peace and justice.

This is simply not true. We need only look at Zimbabwe and America, where we have clearly seen that once certain sources of conflict are removed, new ones emerge.

And while I do not believe whites are superior to blacks, I also do not believe that blacks are more just than whites.

I do not want to hold our politicians and political journalists responsible for all or most of the over-simplifications which interpret conflict as unidimensional. Anybody involved in an action program is tempted to present the problem in simple terms, to look for simple causes and to propose simple remedies. Simple political slogans are easy to sell the public and uninformed masses.

In a paper presented at a recent workshop of the Centre for Intergroup Studies in Cape Town, Ian Liebenberg (1986) presented disturbing evidence of how the local newspapers in Cape Town reinforce and perpetuate the political divisions propagated by the politicians and politically inspired community leaders and demagogues. South African society is complex and it has a heterogenous population — it is not only divided in terms of race and class. Conflict is multidimensional. But demagogues tend to reduce the situation to single factors and present their own side as white and that of the opponent as black. They do not allow for shades of grey, for common ground, or for reconciliation. It is obvious that there are no simple remedies or solutions. The removal of apartheid or the demolition of exploitative capitalism will not ensure a Utopia.

Structural and ideological sources of conflict

Conflict can be due to structural and ideological sources. Structural conflict is usually defined in terms of competition for economic resources, political power and social status. When competition becomes too intense or gets out of hand, it may lead to violence.

Ideological conflict refers to a conflict of ideologies, values, beliefs and perceptions. Goals, interests and values (such as race discrimination, apartheid, capitalism, communism) can acquire ideological meaning and may motivate people to act independently of their objective structural position or interests.

For that reason, whites will oppose apartheid, and privileged people in a capitalist society may propagate communism; British working-class people will support the Conservative and not the Labour Party.

We cannot decide on ways of resolving the conflict without knowing the sources of conflict. It would be fatal to either over-emphasize or ignore any of the more important structural or ideological sources. Ideological commitment usually leads to excessive intolerance, oversimplifications, polarisation and refusal to compromise or reconcile. Ideologies reduce flexible, complicated life situations to rigid, stark, irreconcilable alternatives and promote paranoia.

We have no dearth of ideologies in South Africa. For decades millions of people have suffered from the evils of a system motivated by the granite wall of apartheid. Are we heading for more reasonable political behavior now that this apartheid ideology is waning, or are we heading for another equally evil or worse kind of fanaticism?

New structural and ideological divisions and alliances

The new tri-cameral Parliament has set South African political parties on new paths. The new politics in South Africa have cut across traditional race lines of conflict and have brought new divisions within race groups.

The essential values annd motivating forces that are holding together the major political configurations are changing and these processes lead to new alignments. The establishment used to be motivated by the wish to retain white purity and privilege and used to be exclusively white.

The emerging establishment is less motivated by the traditional apartheid ideology and is more motivated by a business ideology of a free market and efficiency. It is thus incorporating interest groups that share these values, regardless of their racial characteristics. (Hund and Van der Merwe, 1986) Some observers argue that 'There has been a shift from the religious-political ideology of the manifest destiny of the Afrikaner to a more pragmatic, secular ideology of white survival which has necessitated making concessions to non-Afrikaner whites to coloreds and to Asians, and even to urban blacks' (Leatt, Kneifel, Nürnberger, 1986:81).

As the nature of the establishment is changing, the nature of the traditional opposition groups are changing and new opposition groups are emerging. Opposition groups that used to rally support around anti-apartheid issues are increasingly basing their policy on more economic issues.

At present, parliamentary (and most legal) politics are conducted within a broad socio-economic system, which has been and will continue to be accepted rather uncritically by both establishment and current parliamentary opposition parties.

But the legitimacy of this system and of the groups operating within it is increasingly being challenged by interest groups that are operating outside the parliamentary system.

As this system is itself becoming the basic issue, the opposition within the framework becomes less relevant and becomes merged with the establishment in defense against the onslaught to the system.

The establishment used to be exclusively white and the opposition black, indicating a conflict of race. This situation is in flux with the incorporation of black elements in economic, political and social structures. The basic issue is changing in character and so are the components of both the establishment and the opposition. It is useful to handle this state of flux within a framework that distinguishes between three major alliances of interest groups:

(a) *The establishment* is predominantly white and caters for white interests. It is, however, gradually incorporating black components and is increasingly catering for the interests of blacks as well as whites who have a commitment to and a vested interest in the protection of the prevailing socio-economic system.

It includes the major white parties and to an increasing extent the colored and Indian parties participating in the new constitutional dispensation.

In a peripheral sense it also includes African bodies such as Community Councils operating under relatively rigid government control.

(b) *The official or traditional opposition*, including parliamentary opposition and other groups such as business and trade unions who have opposed the Government on race issues, but are willing to co-operate *within the broad socio-economic system of the free market*. As the major thrust of the Government is shifting, this group is also undergoing change. Some elements within this group find themselves more in sympathy with the Government as it removes race discrimination and takes a firmer stand in favor of free enterprise.

To an extent this includes the Progressive Federal Party (PFP), big business, the Trade Union Council of South Africa (Tucsa) and the colored and Indian parties and African councils mentioned above. It also includes the KwaZulu Legislative Assembly and Inkatha. Seen from within the current political system they constitute the opposition to the ruling National Party. But seen within the total setting of South Africa they are becoming part of the establishment.

(c) *Opposition operating outside the current socio-economic and political framework*. They fall outside the framework in two respects:

- -- They are excluded from and/or refuse to participate in the current political structures created by the Government, such as the Parliament, the President's Council, Community Councils and homeland governments.
- — They reject the predominant free market socio-economic system and favor a more socialist system, industrial democracy or related systems.

This category includes organizations such as the United Democratic Front (UDF), the Congress of South African Trade Unions (Cosatu), the National Forum, Azapo, the Pan Africanist Congress (PAC) and the African National Congress (ANC).

They see the basic issues not so much in racial terms but in socio-economic terms. They want a fundamental change of the socio-economic system along somewhat socialist lines. They see the PFP, TUCSA, Inkatha and such organizations as part of the capitalist establishment.

This third group is emerging as the major future opposition group in South Africa, which in time will oppose the regrouped establishment which will probably include Nationalists, Inkatha leaders and the PFP.

The incorporation of colored people and Indians into the central Parliament and the prospects of some kind of accommodation of Africans in the Government in the near future are evidence that race ceases to be the major criterion for discrimination and division in our society. New alliances across racial lines and new divisions within racial groups suggest that there are issues other than race that constitute sources of division among some and grounds for common cause among others.

It is my distinct impression that those blacks who give cautious consideration to some kind of compromise and participation are those relatively favorably disposed towards the socio-economic system of the free market.

This will include those groups that I classified as opposition willing to operate within the present socio-economic framework. They will assist in fundamental political change but will not demand a switch to a socialist economic system.

Equally, those who are more favorably disposed towards a more socialist system (or who are merely anti-capitalist) will be less inclined to participate in the system. Thus the major political division of the future will not be between whites and blacks, but between those who adhere to or propagate the free market ideology and the proponents of a more socialist ideology.

The extent to which their policies, practices and strategies will conform to their ideologies will remain a matter of ongoing debate.

The Government, while pretending to be a major proponent of free enterprise is often accused of merely paying lip-service to this system. The ANC, on the other hand, while being 'formally committed to socialism', is 'hardly doctrinaire' about it (Lodge, 1985:84). 'The main source of radical pressure or influence on the ANC leadership does not come either from its eastern bloc allies or, as is often asserted, from its members who are also communists. With the renaissance of popular political culture during the post-Soweto era there has developed a profound and widespread antipathy to capitalism (Lodge, 1985:84).

The espousal of a certain ideology by one side is often based primarily on the aversion for or a total rejection of the ideology and policy of the opponent. It is more of a negative counter-ideology than a positive commitment.

I suggest, therefore, that in our search for the constructive accommodation of conflict in South Africa, we assess the prospects of communication, dialogue, negotiation and comparatively peaceful settlement of differences between the two major emerging groups: the Establishment and the Extra-Parliamentary Opposition.

I refer to two broad movements which do not constitute unified or uniform groups or parties. There are, in fact, major strains and conflicts within these groups (such as between the HNP and the National Party and between the ANC and the PAC). But within the broader South African political context the major and more crucial problem of conflict and the need for communication will be between the Establishment and the Extra-Parliamentary Opposition.

The Establishment

The Nationalist Government is committed to negotiate. The State President has stated his personal commitment to negotiate several times since August 1985. On 30 September 1985 he stated:

'I thus finally confirm that my Party and I are committed to the principle of a united South Africa, one citizenship and a universal franchise within structures chosen by South Africans. . . .'

'It is the conviction of this Government that the structures in which this co-operation will take place, must be the result of negotiation with the leaders of all the communities'.

If the State President is honest and sincere — and I firmly believe that he is — these statements, which have been repeated in the current Parliamentary session, mean inevitably that he must talk not only to those leaders that have so far been willing to participate in structures imposed by the government, but also to those who have, until now, withheld participation.

It means, in my view, that he must and will talk to the leaders of the UDF, Azapo, the ANC and the PAC. These organizations represent vast masses of South Africans of all communities. No stable, lasting settlement can be worked out without their cooperation. I believe that the State President is aware of that.

Why then, is there no progress? One has reason to be sceptical, especially if the Government does not even make much headway with Chief Buthelezi, the leader of the largest political party in the country and a man who risks his own credibility in his efforts to come to terms with the Government, and to make compromises.

Now that the State President has publicly stated that he is committed to power sharing (see especially his prominent newspaper advertisements), indications are that Inkatha may participate in negotiations that may lead to new national political structures.

Such a development will confirm my argument that the major political divisions in this country are no longer between whites and blacks. We are entering the post-apartheid era with major new divisions.

Assuming that, given the total political spectrum, the channels of communication between the Government and Inkatha are relatively open, I shall discuss the problems of communication between the Establishment and the broad anti-capitalist Extra-Parliamentary Opposition.

Problems of communication

It is my conviction, based especially on personal contact and observation, that important leaders from both camps are not only interested in, but keen to arrive at a negotiated settlement, rather than to continue warfare, sabotage and violence.

While there is an underlying willingness to negotiate, there are several reasons why the Government does not make much progress.

I shall discuss three:

(a) divergent and conflicting trends within the Government,
(b) the perpetration of political violence,
(c) the fear of communism.

Trends within the Government

The *pragmatic* approach, also known as verligtheid, prevails in the dominant circles led by the State President. Their major motivating forces are no longer the Verwoerdian apartheid ideology, but more pragmatic considerations about the maintenance of law and order, the increase in production (especially in a free market economic system), and the maintenance of civilized Western standards. These considerations often require the sacrifice of a number of sacred cows.

In short, the pragmatists have come to realise that if they, as whites, want to *retain any* power, they have to *share* it with blacks.

But not all adherents to the *apartheid ideology* have left the National Party. Not even the verligtes can free themselves so easily from the social forces that have shaped their views for so many decades and generations. The National Party has retained a number of very prominent leaders who are still motivated by the primary aim of maintaining *white* identity and protecting white privilege. This group adheres to the idea of white baasskap and is not interested in a negotiated settlement.

Another important element within the Party and the Government that blocks a negotiated settlement is what I would like to call the *Anti-Communist lobby*. They believe that South Africa is a prime target of the imperial Soviet Communist Onslaught. In response to the perceived 'Total Onslaught', the 'Total Strategy' has been formulated. Firm believers in the 'Total Strategy' leave no room for negotiations with opposition groups that are seen as front organizations for the Communists.

While I have referred to 'individuals' and 'groups' among Nationalists representing apartheid and anti-Communism, it should be noted that no white, Afrikaner or Nationalist, can easily or completely outgrow the conservative social forces that have shaped his life. As Alan Paton put it so aptly: P.W. Botha has to face not only the right wing in the Conservative Party, but also in his own party — and in his own heart.

In spite of the formidable opposition of these two ideologically motivated groups — the apartheid supporters and the anti-communists — I still believe that the present Government under the leadership of Mr P.W. Botha will proceed in its attempts to negotiate. It is morally committed to do so.

It is conceivable that the pragmatists will rely on colored and Indian support to make up for the loss of white support to the right wing. The dissolution of the three present chambers may be a prerequisite for accommodating Africans in the central government. I will not be surprised if that happens in 1986.

Violence

I have said earlier that both Government and opposition groups accuse each other of committing violence. Violence is an extreme manifestation of destructive conflict.

While we used to think of violence only in physical terms and as acts committed by those who oppose authority, we have come to realize that force used by the instruments of the State can be interpreted as institutional or structural violence. The effect of structural violence, such as discriminatory customs or legislation, is that the actual realization of human beings is below their potential realization. Structural violence is manifested in a vicious physical form in the demolition of squatter homes during cold winters.

While violence is usually abhorred in public rhetoric, all politicians and virtually the entire Christian Church believe that violence in its most destructive form, warfare, can be justified under certain conditions. The theology of a just war dates back to the early history of almost all Christian churches. 'There is a long and consistent Christian tradition about the use of physical force to defend oneself against aggressors and tyrants. In other words there are circumstances when physical force may be used' (Kairos Theologians, 1985:12).

South African church leaders do not adopt a pacifist stand. This being the position of the churches, it is most unlikely that any political leaders will support pacifism. Like religious leaders, they will *not* in principle renounce it. They will reserve the right to use violence as a last resort.

If they are in power they will use it to maintain law and order or to squash protest, rebellion, armed revolution or invasion by foreign powers. If they are in opposition and they believe that all normal channels of protest have been closed and the Government is completely intransigent, they will resort to violence believing that justice is on their side.

And, depending on the political and moral convictions of the clergy, they will rally behind either those in authority or those in rebellion, arguing that God is on their side.

The deep divisions among theologians are reflected in *The Kairos Document*. In their 'prophetic' theology 'the Kairos theologians attack Church Theology' for using the word 'violence' in the way it is being used in the propaganda of the State (1985:11).

The Kairos Document refers sharply to 'the structural, institutional and unrepentant violence of the State and especially the oppressive and naked violence of the police and the army' (1985:11—12). They object to the implicaton that there is moral equality between the 'ruthless and repressive activities of the State and the desperate attempts of the people to defend themselves (1985:12).

'In practice what one calls "violence" and what one calls "self-defence" seems to depend upon which side one is on. To call all physical force "violence" is to try to be neutral and to refuse to make a judgment about who is right and who is wrong. The attempt to remain neutral in this kind of conflict is futile. Neutrality enables the status quo of oppression (and therefore violence) to continue. It is a way of giving tacit support to the oppressor' (1985:13).

Given this situation, we must accept that neither Government leaders nor ANC leaders will be willing to renouce violence. In January and August 1985, the State President stated that he would be willing to release political prisoners and talk to ANC leaders provided they renounce violence. Understandably, they were not willing to do so.

It should be noted that while several prominent Government leaders in January 1986 repeated this as a condition for talks with the ANC, the State President has not repeated this condition since August 1985. In several subsequent speeches he has stated the condition in much more positive and realistic terms, namely that he is willing to talk to 'people interested in a peaceful solution'.

By not insisting on a condition that cannot be met by the other party, the State President has convinced me of his sincere commitment to negotiate.

The two parties cannot expect each other to renounce violence, but they can insist on conditional and temporary suspension of violence.

The suspension by the Government of mass removals and influx control, some of the most severe forms of structural violence, is further indication of progress towards conditions favorable for negotiations.

In contrast to these progressive developments on the Government side, South African newspapers have reported extensively on the ANC's intentions to step up the armed struggle in South Africa.

One particular feature that aroused the horror of many South Africans was the ANC's reputed decision to focus on soft targets. These reports reinforced the popular opinon among whites that the ANC is merely a terrorist organization and not interested in a negotiated settlement.

I want to make two observations to put the ANC's stand on this issue in perspective.

First, many papers distorted Oliver Tambo's statements at a press conference. 'Contrary to the impression fostered by the South African authorities and their academic supporters (see for example Campbell 1983) the ANC has never employed a policy of indiscriminate terrorism' (Lodge, 1985:86). Tambo did not say they would now go for soft targets, but that 'the distinction between "soft" and "hard" is going to disappear in an intensified confrontation, in an escalating conflict. The question of soft targets was quite out of place during World War II' (Tambo, 1985:44).

Oliver Tambo's stand was thus no different from that of any head of government who conducts modern warfare, whether he be Russian, American or South African. During the Second World War, 34 million innocent civilians — soft targets — were killed as against only 17 million military staff. The two atom bombs dropped by the Americans destroyed primarily innocent civilians — soft targets.

This lack of respect for human life has now been taken so far by the Americans that they are developing the neutron bomb which has the horrible feature that it will kill only human beings, but leave property intact. The Americans already boast that they can kill every Russian citizen forty times over.

Many people regard the intensification of the struggle as an indication that negotiation is ruled out. Quite the contrary may be true. It is normal for parties in conflict to do their very best to increase their bargaining power before negotiations commence. It is also normal for political leaders (both ANC and Government) to publicly denounce negotiations at such times.

At the same time that Tambo announced the intensification of the armed struggle, the National Executive Committee of the ANC in their Political Report referred to recent contacts between the ANC and South African businessmen, journalists, intellectuals and politicians. They did not condemn these contacts, but he clearly stated that such negotiations should be handled with caution. 'It is absolutely vital that our organization and the democratic movement as a whole should be of one mind about this development to ensure that any contact that may be established does not have any negative effects on the development of our struggle' (Political Report, 1986:36).

Tom Lodge (1985:84) observed a 'new note of conciliation' in the ANC since Nkomati. Even Joe Slovo conceded that one day dialogue might well take place: 'There were conditions under which all states or movements must be prepared to negotiate' (Lodge, 1985:85).

It is therefore my considered opinion that the issue of violence as committed by both the Government and the ANC has in fact become more negotiable than before.

The anticipated release of Nelson Mandela in the near future will be a major step towards a negotiated settlement.

The Communist connection

The second major obstacle to negotiations is the Communist connections of the ANC. These connections are emphasized by the anti-communist lobby in the Government. They accuse ANC leaders of being communists and argue that the ANC is a mere front organization for the Soviets and the Communist Party of South Africa.

The Government demands that the ANC must denounce Communism and sever their Communist links as a prerequisite for negotiations.

It is, however, obvious that the Government cannot ask the ANC to renounce unconditionally their allies of several decades. It will have to accept these connections and live with them, just as it is living with our communist-orientated neighboring countries and as Ian Smith is living with Mugabe.

But it is completely misplaced to regard the ANC as a Communist organization. In the Rivonia trial, the State argued that the Freedom Charter was a communist document and that Nelson Mandela was a Communist. The court did not accept either argument.

Mandela personally testified in court that he was a Christian. He confirmed that towards me personally. His warden testified to his Christian commitment in prison. Two clergymen, the Rev Dudley A Moore and Mr Harry Wiggett recently stated in letters to the press that they have served Mandela holy communion and that he was a committed Christian.

The same applies to several leaders of the African National Congress and of the Pan Africanist Congress in exile whom I have met over the past years.

In court, Nelson did not hesitate to state his appreciation for several aspects of the communist system. The same applies to the current leaders of the ANC in exile. They have relationships and ties with the communist world that cannot be denied. But these ties should *not* be allowed to prevent the Government from entering into negotiations with them.

There is no doubt in my mind that the Communists have a strong hold on the ANC in exile. It is the inevitable result of the banning of the ANC from South Africa.

The most efficient step to free the ANC of this hold of the Communist Party and of the imperialist powers of Communism, is to give it an independent power base in South Africa where it has the support of millions of non-Communists and Christians.

In his authoritative article on the current leadership of the ANC, Tom Lodge (1985:96) argues that the ANC's commitment to a new system does not stem from an 'externally-derived Marxist revolutionary conspiracy' but 'comes rather from a popular political tradition of which the ANC is a central component'.

Prospects for the future

Considering the hard-line elements, the hawks, the political demagogues and the fanatics on both sides of the conflict, judging from public statement by both the Government and the ANC, and noting increasing political violence, the prospects for negotiations in our strife-torn society appear bleak indeed.

But if I judge from my personal contacts with leaders of the most important political groups in our country and those in exile, I am more optimistic. There is a genuine underlying wish among most of these leaders to negotiate in order to develop a system of government acceptable to the people of South Africa.

Communication between conflicting groups is essential to relieve the tension and accommodate conflict in South Africa. Recent statements by the State President and by Oliver Tambo and Nelson Mandela leave sufficient room for negotiations on the highest level. A favorable public atmosphere is necessary for such negotiations. In a democratic society it is the duty of every citizen and organization to promote favorable conditions for such negotiations.

While recent polls among whites show resistance to talks, between South Africans and the ANC (*Rapport*, 16 February 1986) there is no doubt that there has been substantial progress in public opinion in South Africa on this matter.

In December 1984 *Beeld*, the largest Afrikaans pro-Government daily paper published two articles pointing out that there is common ground between the National Party and the ANC, and an editorial calling on the Government to talk to the ANC. These articles were based on a personal meeting between the Assistant Editor of *Beeld* with member of the National Executive Committee of the ANC. Talks with the ANC became a topic of open debate in South Africa and several meetings between South African journalists, academics, students and businessmen in fact took place. When the Government prevented the top student leaders of the University of Stellenbosch from visiting the Youth League of the ANC in Lusaka by confiscating their passports, all pro-Government newspapers deplored it and an Afrikaans publisher, Taurus, produced a book *Praat met die ANC* (Talk to the ANC) on this matter (Olivier, 1985).

Another pro-Government paper, *Die Vaderland*, (25—28 June, 1985) published a series of contributions on the Freedom Charter, arguing that it was not all that unacceptable to the Nationalists.

All these developments help to pave the way for eventual official talks which are inevitable.

References

Campbell, Keith (1983), 'Prospects for terrorism in South Africa' *South Africa International* 14: 397—417.

Hund, John and Hendrik W van der Merwe (1986) *Legal Ideology and Politics in South Africa*. New York: University Press of America and Cape Town: Centre for Intergroup Studies.

Kairos, Theologians (1985) *Challenge to the Church — A theological Comment on the Political Crisis in South Africa: The Kairos Document*. Braamfontein: The Kairos Theologians.

Leatt, James, Theo Kneifel and Klaus Nürnburger (eds) (1986), *Contending Ideologies in South Africa*. Grand Rapids: Wm B Eerdmans: Cape Town: David Philip Publisher.

Liebenberg, Ian (1986) 'Conflict and violence in the Peninsula' Paper presented at the First Workshop of the Centre for Intergroup Studies on Community-Authority Relations, Cape Town, 3 March.

Lodge, Tom (1985), 'The Second Consultative Conference of the African National Congress' *South Africa International* 16, no 2 (October): 80—97.

Olivier, Gerrit (ed) (1985), *Praat met die ANC*. Emmarentia: Taurus.

Tambo, Oliver (1985), 'Political Report of the National Executive Committee to the National Consultative Conference, June 1985'. Published p. 6—37 in *Documents of the Second International Consultative Conference of the African National Congress, Zambia, 16—23 June 1985*. Lusaka: African National Congress.

(1985b), 'Press Conference, Lusaka, June 25 1985'. Published pp. 42—46 in *Documents of the Second National Consultative Conference of the African National Congress, Zambia, 16—23 June 1985*. Lusaka: African National Congress.

Die, Vaderland (1985), The Freedom Charter Debate *Die Vaderland*, 25—28 June.

LIST OF PARTICIPANTS AND OBSERVERS

Participants

ADEKOYA, Mr Oluwole (Nigeria), Nigerian High Commission, Dar es Salaam

AICARDI DE SAINT PAUL, Dr Marc (France), Researcher, Author on African Affairs

ANDREWS, Ms Penelope (South Africa), Lecturer, La Trobe University

ARNOLD, Mr Millard W. (USA), President, Associates International, Washington DC

ARNOULD, H.E. Mr D.C. (Canada), High Commissioner of Canada, Dar es Salaam

BANDORA, Mr Musinga (Tanzania), Counsellor — Ministry of Foreign Affairs, Dar es Salaam

BAREGU, Dr M. (Tanzania), Lecturer, UDS

BAVU, Professor I.K. (Tanzania), Head, Department of Political Science, University of Dar es Salaam

BRSCIC, Mr Marijan (Yugoslavia), Yugoslav Embassy, Dar es Salaam

CAMPBELL, Dr Kurt M. (USA), Research Fellow, Kennedy School of Government, Harvard University

CARR, Canon Burgess (Liberia), International Consultant on Human and Ethical Issues in Africa Development

CHEKA, Mrs Mboni O. (Tanzania) Member of Parliament

CHILAMBO, Mr Luke (Tanzania), Minister Counsellor, Ministry of Foreign Affairs, Dar es Salaam

DASGUPTA, H.E. Mr C. (India), Indian High Commissioner, Dar es Salaam

EKMAN, Mr Andreas (Sweden), Counsellor, Swedish Embassy, Dar es Salaam

FREDERIKSE, Ms Julie (USA), Writer, Broadcaster, Harare

GALAYDH, Dr Ali Khalif (Somalia), Research Fellow, Center for Middle Eastern Studies, Harvard University

GAMBLE, Mr Richard B. (USA), IPA Board Member

GIMONGE, Mr C.K. (Tanzania), Army Officer

HARTMANN, Dr Jeanette (Tanzania), Lecturer, University of Dar es Salaam

HOEKEMA, Mr Jan (Netherlands), Head of Political Affairs Desk, Directorate for Political UN Affairs, Ministry of Foreign Affairs, The Hague

HOKORORO, Dr A.M. (Tanzania), Director, CFR

ITO, Mr Shosuke (Japan), Counsellor, Japanese Embassy, Dar es Salaam

JASTER, Mr Robert (USA), International Institute for Strategic Studies, London

JONAH, Dr James O.C. (Sierra Leone), Assistant Secretary-General for Field Operational and External Support Activities, United Nations

KAMUHANDA, Mr H.S. (Tanzania), Journalist, Tanzania News Agency, Shihata

KIBACHA, Ms H.S. (Tanzania), Principal Assistant Secretary, Chama Cha Mapinduzi, (CCM)

KIBOLA, Mr H. (Tanzania), Lecturer, CFR

KIKWABHA, Mr R.C. (Tanzania), First Secretary, International Relations, Ministry of Foreign Affairs, Dar es Salaam

KOMBE, Maj. Gen. I.H. (Tanzania), Chief of Staff, Tanzania People's Defence Forces

KUHANGA, Mr Nicholas (Tanzania), Vice Chancellor, University of Dar es Salaam

KUNSTADTER, Mrs G. (USA), Vice President, Albert Kundstadter Family Foundation

KUNSTADTER, Mr John (USA), Treasurer, International Peace Academy

LABAM, Mr Christopher (Tanzania), Ministry of Foreign Affairs, Dar es Salaam

LEGUM, Mr Colin (UK), Journalist, UK

LIPUMBA, Dr N.H.I. (Tanzania), Lecturer, University of Dar es Salaam

LISWANI, Mr K. (Namibia), Deputy Chief Representative, SWAPO

MADUNA, Mr P.M. (South Africa), ANC

MAFOLE, Mr I.M. (South Africa), PAC, Administrator

MAGOGO, Mr Crispin (Tanzania), Civil Servant

MAHLAFUNA, Mr Isco (South Africa), ANC

MAKARANGA, Brig. S.A. (Tanzania), Army

MASARO, Mr I.P. (Tanzania), Ministry of Foreign Affairs, Dar es Salaam

MAWALLA, Mr B.M. (Tanzania), Counsellor, Ministry of Foreign Affairs, Dar es Salaam

MCHUMO, H.E. Mr A. (Tanzania), Ambassador of Tanzania to Maputo

MEELA, Mr D.S. (Tanzania), Principal Secretary, Ministry of Justice

MISOMALI, Mr D.D. (Malawi), Malawi High Commission, DSM

MJAALAND, Mr Dag. (Norway), Attaché, Royal Norwegian Embassy, Dar es Salaam

MOKOENA, Mr Raymond (South Africa), ANC

MOTAU, Mr Edgar (South Africa), PAC

MSABAHA, Dr Ibrahim (Tanzania), Director of Studies and Programmes, CFR

MUGANDA, Mr B. (Tanzania), Director of Research and Information, Ministry of Foreign Affairs, Dar es Salaam

MUNGOMA, Ms Lucy (Zambia), Ministry of Foreign Affairs, Lusaka, Zambia

MWAITENDA, Mr A.A.B. (Tanzania), Commissioner of Police

MWANSASU, Mr W. (Tanzania), Senior Supt. of Police

NGWENYA, Mr P. (Zimbabwe), Zimbabwe High Commission

NOLUTSHUNGU, Mr S. (UK), Department of Government, University of Manchester

OGUNSANWO, Prof. A. (Nigeria), Dept of Political Science and Public Administration, University of Lagos

OYAKA, Mr Laban (Uganda), OAU, Dar es Salaam

PANGALIS, Mrs Celia S. (USA), Director of Conflict Resolution Studies, IPA

RENDOH, Mr David (Botswana), Counsellor, Botswana High Commission, Lusaka

RIKHYE, Major General Indar Jit (India), President, International Peace Academy

RISTIMAKI, H.E. Mr Ilkka (Finland), Ambassador of Finland, United Republic of Tanzania, Dar es Salaam

Rucker-Kirschner, Mr J. (FRG), Embassy of the Federal Republic of Germany, Dar es Salaam

RUPIA, Ambassador Paul (Tanzania), Principal Secretary, Ministry of Foreign Affairs, Dar es Salaam

SASTOURNE, Mr François (France), First Secretary, French Embassy, Dar es Salaam

SHEMNDOLWA, Mr S.A. (Tanzania), Police Officer

SHIHEPO, Mr Aaron (Namibia), Deputy Secretary, Foreign Affairs Department, SWAPO

STREMLAU, Dr John (USA), Associate Director, International Relations, Rockefeller Foundation, New York

SUTHERLAND, Dr Bill (USA), Recently, Fellow Institute of Politics, Kennedy School of Government

SWAI, Colonel F.S. (Tanzania), Army

TIBANDEBAGE, Mr Richard (Tanzania), Civil Servant

VAN DER MERWE, Prof, H. Willem (South Africa), Director, Centre for Intergroup Studies

VENGESAYI, Mr C.R. (Zimbabwe), Zimbabwe High Commission

WEISS, Dr T.G. (USA), Executive Vice President, International Peace Academy

Observers

ADADI, R. (Tanzania), Police Officer

BISWARO, J.M. (Tanzania), Diplomat Trainee

FREIER, Dr Rolf (FRG), Representative, Friedrich Naumann Foundation

HAUKONGO, F.M. (Namibia), Diplomat Trainee

KAIJAGE, M.B. (Tanzania), Diplomat Trainee

KALLAGHE, P.A. (Tanzania), Diplomat Trainee

KAPWERA, M.K. (Tanzania), Diplomat Trainee

KIMBWEREZA, E.D. (Tanzania), Diplomat Trainee

LYARUU, E.J. (Tanzania), Diplomat Trainee

MAMBOLEO, Mr. K. (Tanzania)

MANDARI, S. (Tanzania), Diplomat Trainee

MATIKU, N.M. (Tanzania), Diplomat Trainee

MUNDI, M.O. (Tanzania), Diplomat Trainee

MBATIA, W.M.C. (Tanzania), Diplomat Trainee

MBOTI, L.J. (Namibia), Diplomat Trainee

MTENGETI, R.N. (Tanzania), Diplomat Trainee

MWAKASEGE, V. (Tanzania), Diplomat Trainee

NYANGE, J. (Tanzania), Diplomat Trainee

SEFUE, O. (Tanzania), Diplomat Trainee

SEMGURUKA, L.P. (Tanzania), Diplomat Trainee

SHAO, R.A. (Tanzania), Diplomat Trainee

Secretariat

GONDWE, Mr. C.H.M. (Tanzania), Lecturer, Centre for Foreign Relations, Dar es Salaam

HOUSE, Ms. Charlotte (U.K.), Associate Program Officer, International Peace Academy, New York

JENGO, Mrs. R.D. (Tanzania), Librarian, Centre for Foreign Relations, Dar es Salaam

KASHONDA, Mrs. M.M. (Tanzania), Lecturer, Centre for Foreign Relations

KASSIM, Ms. S. (Tanzania), University of Dar es Salaam

KAUDE, Mrs. M. (Tanzania), Personal Secretary, Centre for Foreign Relations, Dar es Salaam

MAKUMULO, Mr. A. (Tanzania), Lecturer, Centre for Foreign Relations, Dar es Salaam

NYANGE, Mr. A.L. (Tanzania), Lecturer, Centre for Foreign Relations, Dar es Salaam

APPENDIX I

United Nations Security Council Resolution 435 (1978)

Adopted by the Security Council at its 2087th meeting on 29 September 1978

The Security Council,

Recalling its resolutions 385 (1976) and 431 (1978), and 432 (1978),

Having considered the report submitted by the Secretary-General pursuant to paragraph 2 of resolution 431 (1978) (S/12827) and his explanatory statement made in the Security Council on 29 September 1978 (S/12869),

Taking note of the relevant communications from the Government of South Africa addressed to the Secretary-General,

Taking note also of the letter dated 8 September 1978 from the President of the South West Africa People's Organization (SWAPO) addressed to the Secretary-General (S/12841),

Reaffirming the legal responsibility of the United Nations over Namibia,

1. *Approves* the report of the Secretary-General (S/12827) for the implementation of the proposal for a settlement of the Namibian situation (S/12636) and his explanatory statement (S/12869);

2. *Reiterates* that its objective is the withdrawal of South Africa's illegal administration of Namibia and the transfer of power to the people of Namibia with the assistance of the United Nations in accordance with resolution 385 (1976);

3. *Decides* to establish under its authority a United Nations Transition Assistance Group (UNTAG) in accordance with the above-mentioned report of the Secretary-General for a period of up to 12 months in order to assist his Special Representative to carry out the mandate conferred upon him by paragraph 1 of Security Council resolution 431 (1978), namely, to ensure the early independence of Namibia through free and fair elections under the supervision and control of the United Nations;

4. *Welcomes* SWAPO's preparedness to co-operate in the implementation of the Secretary-General's report, including its expressed readiness to sign and observe the cease-fire provisions as manifested in the letter from the President of SWAPO dated 8 September 1978 (S/12841);

5. *Calls on* South Africa forthwith to co-operate with the Secretary-General in the implementation of this resolution;

6. *Declares* that all unilateral measures taken by the illegal administration in Namibia in relation to the electoral process, including unilateral registration of voters, or transfer of power, in contravention of Security Council resolutions 385 (1976), 431 (1978) and this resolution are null and void;

7. *Requests* the Secretary-General to report to the Security Council no later than 23 October 1978 on the implementation of this resolution.

APPENDIX II

List of abbreviations

ANC	African National Congress of South Africa
BLS	Botswana, Lesotho, Swaziland
CFR	Centre for Foreign Relations
CONSAS	Constellation of Southern African States
COSATU	Congress of South African Trade Unions
CUSA	Council of Unions of South Africa
DRC	Dutch Reformed Church
ECA	(United Nations) Economic Commission for Africa
EEC	European Economic Community
FLS	Frontline States
FRG	Federal Republic of Germany
FOSATU	Federation of South African Trade Unions
FRELIMO	Frente de Libertaccao de Mocambique
GDP	Gross Domestic Product
GNP	Gross National Product
IPA	International Peace Academy
LN	League of Nations
MPC	Multi-Party Conference
MPLA	Movimento Popular de Libertacao de Angola
MNR	Mozambique National Resistance (Renamo)
NUM	National Union of Mineworkers
OAU	Organization of African Unity
OECD	Organization for Economic Cooperation and Development
PAC	Pan African Congress

PFP	Progressive Federal Party
PRA	People's Republic of Angola
PTA	Preferential Trade Agreement
RSA	Republic of South Africa
SACC	South African Council of Churches
SADCC	Southern African Development Coordination Committee
SACTU	South African Congress of Trade Unions
SACU	Southern African Customs Union
SADF	South African Defence Forces
SWAPO	South West Africa People's Organization
UK	United Kingdom
UN	United Nations
UNDP	United Nations Development Programme
UNITA	National Union for the Total Independence of Angola
UNTAG	United Nations Transition Assistance Group
US	United States of America
USSR	Union of Soviet Socialist Republics
WCC	World Council of Churches
ZANU	Zimbabwe African National Union

ABOUT THE INTERNATIONAL PEACE ACADEMY

The International Peace Academy (IPA) is a non-profit, non-governmental, academic training institute established to teach the skills of peacekeeping, peacemaking and peacebuilding to mid-career diplomats and military officers on a global basis. Since 1970, over 3,500 diplomats, military officers, policy-makers and academicians from 131 nations have attended IPA training seminars in Africa, Asia, Europe, North and Latin America.

Main activities of the Academy are:

- **design and organization of** *international training seminars* **in peacekeeping and peacemaking to prepare professionals in crisis management**
- **initiation and administration of** *off-the-record meetings* **between disputing parties to facilitate their discussions**
- *publication* **of reports and books related both to practical experience and to scholarly** *research* **to identify options for resolving conflicts**

The IPA is wholly transnational in its Board of Directors and program and administrative staff. Its financial support comes from foundation and corporate grants, private individuals and tuition fees of governments. All contributions in the United States and Canada are tax-deductible.

For further information on the Academy and its programs, contact:

The International Peace Academy, 777 United Nations Plaza, New York, NY 10017, Tel: (212) 949 8480

ABOUT THE CENTRE FOR FOREIGN RELATIONS

The Centre for Foreign Relations (CFR) was established in 1978 by an agreement between the governments of Mozambique and Tanzania. The Centre provides training for government officers from countries in the region, to promote social, economic and political awareness through the study of international affairs and training in the principles, procedures and techniques of diplomacy. The Centre engages in research projects and sponsors conferences and seminars from time to time.

ABOUT THE UNIVERSITY OF DAR ES SALAAM

The University of Dar es Salaam was established in 1970 following the decision by the East African Authority to expand the University of East Africa into three independent universities serving the needs of Tanzania, Uganda and Kenya, respectively. Academic cooperation and communication between the three institutions is maintained through the International University Committee for East Africa. There are currently approximately 4,000 enrolled at the University of Dar es Salaam.